Goldwork AND
Silk Shading
INSPIRED BY NATURE

Dedication to Hazel

This book is dedicated to the memory of my darling wife Hazel, who was such a talented and inspirational embroiderer, and a friend to all her many students.

Without the help and support of Jan Barsby, this book would not have been possible – Hazel was still finishing off the manuscript for the book when she was so suddenly taken from us in 2018. Jan trained at the Royal School of Needlework as an apprentice a year behind Hazel and their friendship goes back a long time. Jan also assisted Hazel with her larger classes in the last couple of years, and they spent a lot of time discussing Hazel's plans for this book. We are very fortunate that Jan was able to pick up from Hazel's notes and designs to finish off what Hazel had started.

ADRIAN RICHARDS

Hazel was a truly inspirational teacher. She encouraged all her students to achieve their best. Her lessons were fun and her enthusiasm was infectious. She not only taught her students how to embroider but to love and be proud of what they achieved. Her talent as a goldworker and teacher was unmatched and she will be very much missed.

JAN BARSBY

Goldwork AND Silk Shading

INSPIRED BY NATURE

Hazel Everett

Search Press

Suppliers
If you have difficulty in obtaining any of the materials and
equipment mentioned in this book, then please visit the Search
Press website for details of suppliers: www.searchpress.com

Metric and imperial conversions
The projects in this book have been made using metric
measurements, and the imperial equivalents provided have been
calculated following standard conversion practices. The imperial
measurements are often rounded to the nearest $\frac{1}{16}$in for ease
of use except in rare circumstances; however, if you need more
exact measurements, there are a number of excellent online
converters that you can use. Always use either metric or imperial
measurements, not a combination of both.

Extra copies of the templates are available from
www.bookmarkedhub.com.

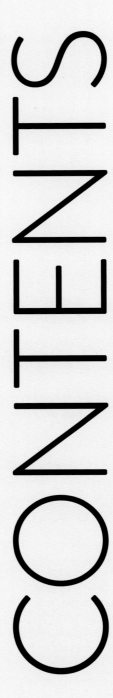

CONTENTS

Acknowledgements

Thank you to the members of the Search Press team who worked
on this book and helped bring it to life:
Roz Dace, Katie French, Becky Robbins, Juan Hayward,
Marrianne Miall and Emma Sutcliffe.

Thank you to the students who helped with the samples:
Elaine Brum, Kate Hedger and Clare Phelan.

Foreword

Sadly, Hazel was taken from us before she was able to finish this book. To make sure that students were still able to benefit from her work and ideas, her husband Adrian and I decided to complete the book, following her plans for it – ensuring that Hazel's vision could continue.

I was lucky enough to train with Hazel at the Royal School of Needlework (RSN), although I was in the year below her. We later worked together at the RSN: Hazel mainly worked in the teaching department, sometimes working on some commissions in the workrooms, while I worked mainly in the workrooms, teaching occasionally. When we left, we often worked on private commissions together. Her passion for goldwork and mine for silk shading made a good combination.

Hazel and I were very different people with differing ideas, but our mutual respect for original techniques and desire for quality results outweighed our differences in design and choice of mediums. We complemented each other and enjoyed working together. In the later years, I was lucky enough to co-teach with Hazel. During this time we talked constantly about the book, and that she wanted it to inspire other embroiderers. I hope that I have been able to finish what she had started in true Hazel style, as an appropriate and fitting tribute to one of my best friends.

Jan Barsby

Introduction

This book covers the techniques I was taught as an apprentice at the RSN when it resided in Princes Gate, Kensington. These are not the only methods available, but I have found them to be very successful. Over the years I have adapted and added my versions to the techniques. Having taught for over 30 years, many questions have cropped up and through this work, together with my students, we have pushed the boundaries. My goldwork embroidery is still technically proficient, but it has also become much freer. The lovely array of colours now available in metal threads has increased dramatically and this has encouraged further experimentation.

Goldwork and silk shading have always been a luxurious combination, often seen in church vestments. The ideas in this book will show that they do not need to be confined to religious work, and will hopefully inspire you to use this combination of techniques in new and innovative ways.

The joy of using a combination of goldwork and silk shading is that your imagination can be set free. It is important to remember your own skill set, as a design that is too large and complicated may prove unachievable and overwhelming. Keep it simple if you are new to the techniques and build up gradually. Draw from your own personal preferences. Inspiration can come from anywhere – from photographs, books, greetings cards and real life, and you can produce a truly unique piece of embroidery by drawing the design yourself. If, however, this is too daunting, you can find designs in books and modify these. Simple designs can be enhanced and complicated designs can be modified.

Experiment and enjoy when designing, but keep a constant thought on how you are going to work each area to achieve your desired effect. Think about the flow of lines, the filling of spaces and the balance of the work. Be realistic and have fun.

Hazel Everett

Equipment

There is very little equipment required for goldwork and silk shading.
You will probably have most items already in your toolbox.

1. Scissors: for goldwork it is best to have a specific pair of scissors for cutting the metal threads, as they can damage the blades. Bent scissors are useful for cutting chips accurately; for general embroidery it is important to have a small, sharp pair of scissors.

2. Stiletto: this is a pointed tool used to create holes in the background fabric through which thick threads can be passed without causing any damage to the fabric. It can also be used to manipulate metal threads when stitching.

3. Mellore: a mellore (or mellor) is a specialist tool used to manoeuvre and manipulate metal threads. The fine pointed end can be used as a stiletto and can also help as a laying tool, aiding in the control of threads. The flat, fat end is used to stroke metal thread – particularly broad plate. It is a very useful but not essential tool.

4. Tweezers: two types are useful: highly pointed to help manipulate metal threads in intricate areas, and flat-ended to tweak metal threads and create the desired effect.

5. Beeswax: this is used to give a light coating to the sewing thread. This adds strength to the thread when attaching metal. It also helps the sewing thread to slide through hollow metals when stitching them down.

6. Velvet board: this is useful to cut purls on as it stabilizes the purl when cutting and keeps it safe whilst waiting to be used (see also page 28). It can also be used as a palette displaying freshly cut pieces of purl.

7. Emery cushion: this cleans needles by removing dirt, impurities and small burrs when needles are pushed in and out of it. They often come in forms such as the strawberry.

8. Cord winder: this is a helpful but not essential tool. It creates cords by winding threads together to form a twist. Cords can also be made by hand (see page 40).

9. Pouncing equipment: this is used for transferring a design onto fabric. The **pricker** is a handle with a screw fitting to hold the needle. It is used to make holes in a design for the pounce to go through. The **pricking mat** is a foam rectangle, which creates a spongy surface to prick on. **Pounce** is pushed through the holes of the design onto the fabric. It is made from powdered chalk (white) and/or charcoal (black). You will need to decide which one shows up best on your chosen fabric. The **pouncer** is felt, rolled up in a tight roll held together with thread. It is used to rub the pounce though the pricked holes onto the fabric.

10. Shade card: this is a piece of thin card with holes, which hold thread samples. The thread name or number can be written next to the threads for easy recognition of the colours in use. This is also a good way to store threads while you are using them.

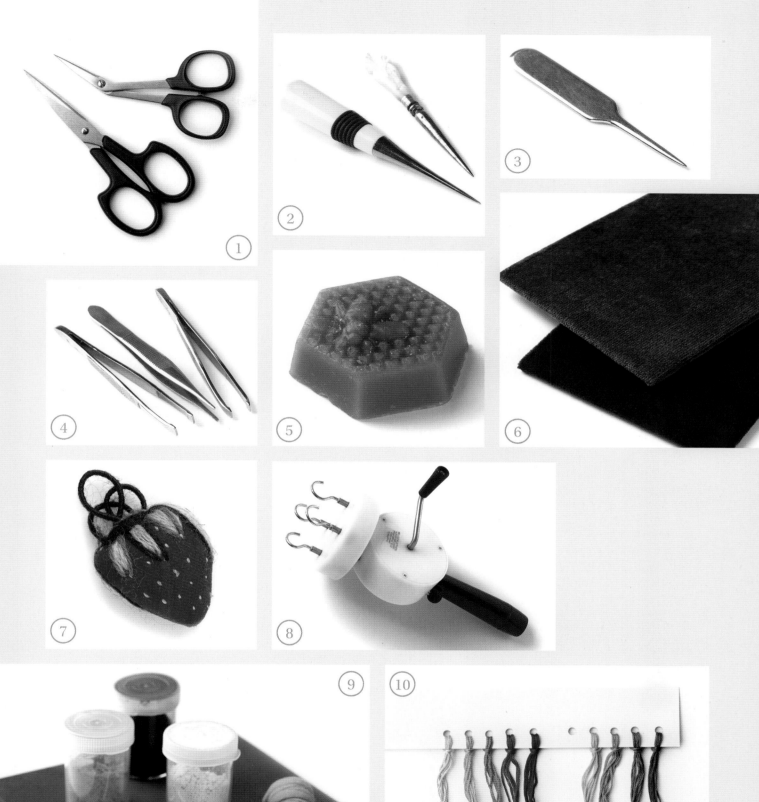
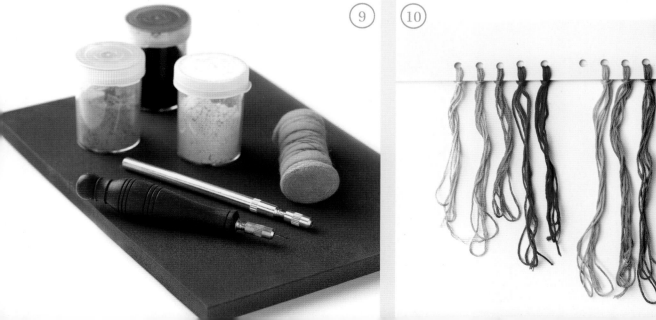

Needles

Needles come in all sizes and the ones listed below are the general ones used for goldwork and silk shading embroidery. Needles can vary with make but a general rule is the larger the number, the smaller the needle.

ESSENTIAL NEEDLES

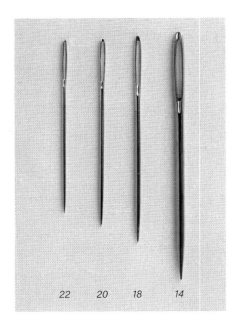

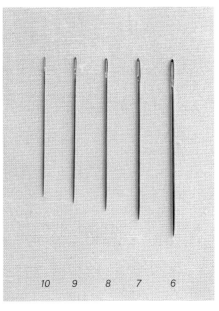

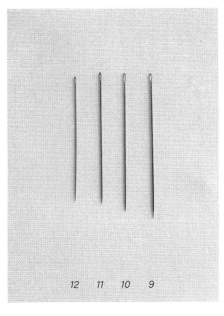

Chenille needle:

Sizes available: no. 13 (largest) to no. 26 (finest).

This is a sturdy needle with a sharp point and slightly bulging eye. This allows thick threads to be accommodated easily. These needles are used when taking thick threads and cords through to the back of the fabric (plunging).

No. 18 is the most popular size.

Crewel needle:

Sizes available: no. 1 (largest) to no. 10 (finest).

This is a fine needle with a long, slightly wider eye and a very sharp point. It can also be referred to as an embroidery needle. It is most frequently used for couching over metal threads and passing through hollow purls in goldwork.

In silk shading it is the most popular needle; the most commonly used sizes are no. 8, no. 9 and no. 10, at the finer end of the range.

Sharps needle:

Sizes available: no. 2 (largest) to no. 10 (finest), but two finer sizes (nos. 11 and 12) are sometimes available.

This is a fine needle with a small round eye and a sharp point. It is ideal for metal threads as it passes through hollow purls with ease, although the small eye can be difficult to thread. It is a good choice when using invisible thread or heavy metal thread.

Nos. 10, 11 and 12 are the most commonly used.

These are not advisable for use in silk shading as the thread can be damaged by the small eye and they are extremely difficult to thread.

USEFUL NEEDLES

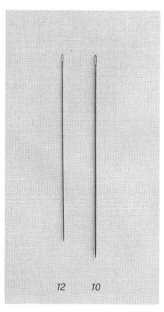

12   10

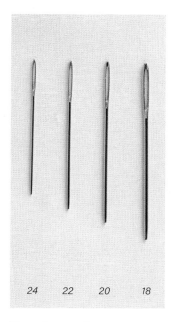

24   22   20   18

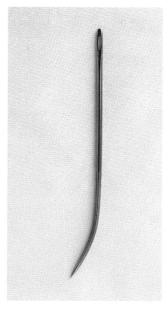

Curved needle:

Sizes available: several sizes can be purchased including large, curved upholstery needles (above right) and fine, curved beading needles (above left).

This is semi-circular in shape and is very useful for working in rigid, flat areas. The larger sizes are good for lacing up finished embroideries over card (see page 23). The smaller sizes are good for delicate work like stitching cords around small pillow decorations or for fine repair work.

Curved needles can feel strange to hold at first, but they are extremely useful once mastered.

Beading needle:

Sizes available: no. 10 (largest) to no. 15 (finest).

This is an extremely long, fine needle with a narrow, oblong eye. It is very useful for going through longer lengths of hollow purls, especially when attaching purl rings around stones as the needle needs to pass through the purl twice. Polyester sewing thread passes through the narrow eye easily.

Straw needles (also known as Milliners) make a good alternative to beading needles for attaching purl. They are basically very long sharps needles.

Tapestry needle:

Sizes available: no. 13 (largest) to no. 28 (finest).

This is similar to a chenille needle but with a blunt point. It is a sturdy needle with a large, elongated, slightly bulging eye. This allows multiple or thick threads to be accommodated, so it is ideal for taking ends through to the wrong side of the fabric once a hole has been made using a stiletto or mellore (see page 8). Tapestry needles are more readily available than chenille needles, which is why they have been included here. No. 13 is an extremely large needle and can be used with string to lace up the side of a frame.

Bracing needle:

Sizes available: usually available in only one size.

This is more unusual in shape, being a very large needle with a spear-shaped, curved point and a wide eye. It may also be referred to as a packing, upholstery or sailmaker's needle. Its main use is with string to dress a slate frame (see pages 14–15).

Fabrics

Almost any fabric can be used for goldwork and silk shading embroidery. However, the fabric does need to be fairly firm and reasonably closely woven to take the weight of the embroidery.

Silk dupion is a popular choice as it is 'embroiderer-friendly.' It holds the embroidery well and comes in a beautiful array of colours, many of which are shot (one colour for the weft and another for the warp), giving added interest. It is also relatively easy to purchase.

Choice of fabric colour depends on personal preference and the purpose of the embroidery. The colour can dramatically affect the overall appearance of the embroidery. Both goldwork and silk shading sit well on darker colours as they can add an elegance to the overall effect. On the other hand, lighter shades highlight darker colours and can add to the design itself, enhancing the finished embroidery.

Smooth or slightly textured fabrics are easier to embroider on. They are therefore suitable for all levels of embroiderer. Highly textured fabrics and extremely textured fabrics such as velvet require padding to prevent the embroidery from sinking and disappearing. I would not recommend highly textured fabrics to a beginner as whilst the textures can enhance the overall embroidery, the challenge they pose to the embroiderer mean that they are extremely difficult to work on.

Whatever fabric is chosen, it needs to be stable enough to support the weight of the embroidery. To achieve extra stability a support layer can be added as a background fabric. Good options for this can be pre-shrunk calico (used on the samples throughout this book) or iron-on backing paper. It is always best to support large designs with a backing. Throughout this book all the embroideries have been worked on silk dupion.

A selection of fabrics suitable for use with goldwork and silk shading.

12

Frames

It is always best to work goldwork and silk shading on taut fabric. This is achieved using frames. Frames help to support the fabric and keep a good tension when working to avoid the base fabric puckering. There are a wide variety of frames available, both round and square. It is best to use what is right for you. You may need to consider whether you intend to work in one place or if your work needs to be portable. How big is the design you are working on: will it fit in a ring frame or does it need a square frame? Where and when are you working on it: is there space in the area for a large square frame?

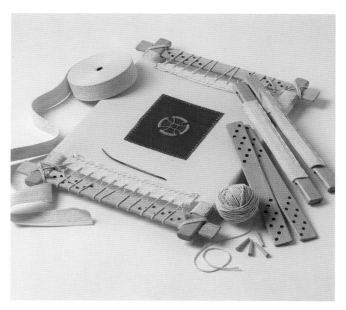

A dressed slate frame and a display of all the individual components for a second frame, including bars, arms, webbing, string, pegs and a bracing needle.

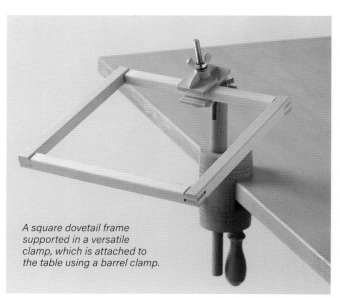

A square dovetail frame supported in a versatile clamp, which is attached to the table using a barrel clamp.

SQUARE OR RECTANGULAR FRAMES

SLATE FRAMES

These come in many sizes and are versatile as the size can be altered during the embroidery. They consist of two rollers/bars with a strip of webbing nailed along an edge, two arms with holes drilled at regular intervals and four pegs. They hold the fabric extremely taut and can be extended if the fabric relaxes. It takes time to prepare for the embroidery but it is worth it (see dressing a square frame on page 14). They can be heavy and need adequate support such as trestles.

SQUARE FRAMES

Square frames are perfect for large projects. They can be cumbersome so need a firm support such as trestles. These frames do not damage the background fabric and allow a large working area. They come in various sizes but have fixed sides, which can limit what they are used for.

ROTATING OR TRAVEL FRAMES

These consist of two rollers that clip to the top and bottom of the arms. They are secured by screws and can loosen over time. They are limited in size and therefore only suitable for small or narrow pieces of work.

DOVETAIL FRAMES

These consist of four bars with dovetail joints interlocking with each other. The fabric is attached with drawing pins or 3-point silk pins. They are very light but it is difficult to get the fabric taut.

VERSATILE CLAMP

This is used in conjunction with a stand or table clamp. There is a dowel with a clamp attached to it. The dowel goes into a hole in the stand or table for support. The clamp holds the frame in place, but this only works if it is a light frame.

DRESSING A SLATE FRAME

'Dressing a frame' is the term used to describe mounting fabric in a frame ready for embroidery. The method illustrated below is the traditional way of mounting calico in a slate frame and attaching the background fabric to the calico.

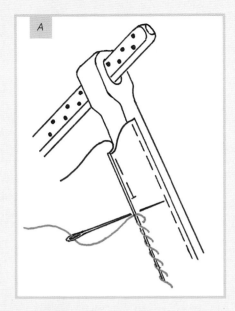

EQUIPMENT

- Slate frame
- Background fabric
- Pre-shrunk calico, larger than the background fabric
- Bracing needle or large tapestry needle
- Assorted needles, including a crewel no. 6
- 4cm (1½in) wide webbing or twill tape
- Light-coloured buttonhole thread
- Scissors for cutting threads
- Pencil
- Pins

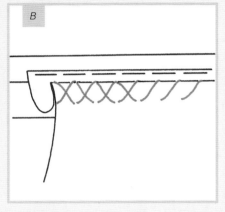

ORDER OF WORK

1 Mark the centre of each roller with the pencil on the webbing. For greater accuracy measure the actual rollers, as the webbing is often misaligned.

2 Make a 13mm (½in) fold along the top and bottom edges of the calico.

3 Measure and mark with a pin the centre of each folded edge. With the wrong side of the fabric facing the underside of the webbing, match the centre marks and pin into place. Work from the centre outwards in each direction. This should produce a ridge effect that is strong and easier to oversew along.

4 Using buttonhole thread, oversew the edge of the fabric to the edge of the webbing, working from the centre outwards (**A**). Make the stitches approximately 6mm (¼in) wide and deep, and stitch to the end of the webbing. Now re-stitch over the sewn edge for about 2.5cm (1in) and then fasten off. This gives added strength to a very weak area (**B**). Repeat this with the second roller.

5 Now insert the arms into the channels at the end of each roller. Take care to insert the arms so that they lie in opposite directions to each other (**C**). This helps keep an even tension. Next, insert the pegs into the most appropriate holes in the arms to make the frame taut. Check that the pegs are in corresponding holes on each side. Measure the distance along the arms between the two rollers on both sides to check that they match. Keep the frame slightly loose at the moment. A background fabric must be applied to loose fabric, otherwise when the work is complete and removed from the frame, the calico will 'relax' and pucker up the background fabric.

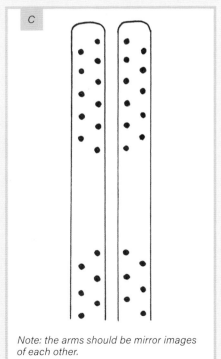

Note: the arms should be mirror images of each other.

6 Sometimes it is necessary to roll up some of the fabric onto one of the rollers. When this is needed, roll a protective cover up with the fabric and bring it up and over the roller. This will stop the edge of the background fabric from becoming marked.

7 Place a strip of webbing along each exposed edge of the fabric so that the webbing overlaps the fabric by half its width. Pin and then attach the webbing to the fabric with a diagonal basting stitch using buttonhole thread.

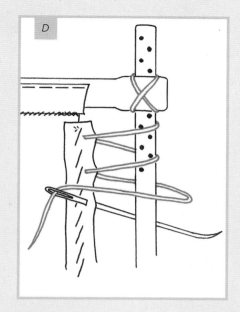

8 Using the bracing needle or large tapestry needle, lace through the webbing and around the arms. Always stand up and point the needle down into the webbing to avoid injury when lacing a frame (**D**). Lace up both sides and then tighten the strings, checking that the channels between the webbing and arm are even. Keep a loose tension at the moment, otherwise it will affect the background fabric when it is applied. Tie off the ends of the string.

9 Support the frame over trestles or with other stands. Lay the background fabric over the suspended calico. Check that the grain is straight and that it is in the centre of the calico. Place a pin in the middle of each side to stabilize the fabric. Now, working from the middle out, pin each side. It is best to pin opposite edges rather than working around the shape as this helps to keep the tension even.

10 Attach the background fabric to the calico either with long and short stitches (**E**) or herringbone stitch (**F**). Again, it is best to work from the middle out on opposite sides first and then repeat this for the remaining opposite edges.

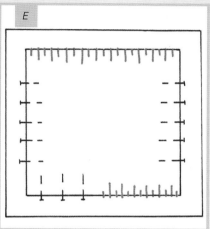

11 Tighten the frame by moving the pegs out. Check the distance by counting the holes and measuring between the pegs on each side with a tape measure. Pull up the lacing until the fabric is as taut as possible, ideally drum tight.

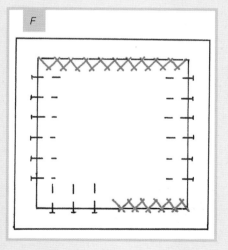

A dressed frame.

HOOPS AND RING FRAMES

These, as the name suggests, are round frames, and they hold the fabric between two rings put together. They come in a wide range of sizes and quality. It is better to spend a little bit more money and buy a frame that has a screw on the top ring to tighten the ring to hold in the fabric. The best hoops to use are wide wood, as they keep a good tension and can be further tightened with a screwdriver.

These are ideal for small projects. They are easy to transport, quick to put together and will keep the fabric reasonably taut when working the embroidery. Unfortunately, when the fabric is crushed between the two rings it can cause damage to the fabric by marking it. To help minimize this, it can help to remove the piece of work from the frame after each embroidery session. It is also a good idea to wrap the outer hoop with torn strips of calico or bias binding to protect the right side of the fabric. This helps keep the background fabric clean and also aids grip, helping to maintain a good firm tension. If possible, you should try to use a ring that is much larger than the whole design so that any damage to the background fabric will not be seen when the embroidery is finished.

If at all possible, to enable you to sew with both hands and not to have to hold your frame, it is advisable to get a hoop with a dowel attached as this will allow it to be supported in a barrel, seat base or free-standing base. Alternatively, a versatile clamp could be used, but this is less stable.

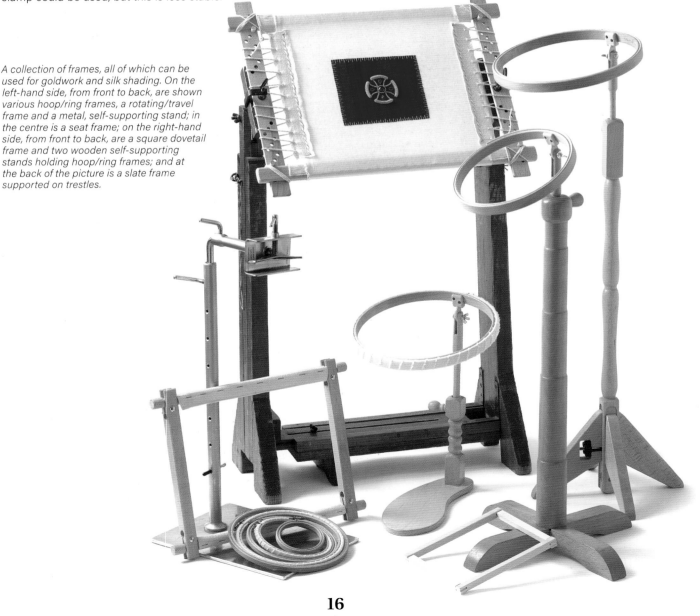

A collection of frames, all of which can be used for goldwork and silk shading. On the left-hand side, from front to back, are shown various hoop/ring frames, a rotating/travel frame and a metal, self-supporting stand; in the centre is a seat frame; on the right-hand side, from front to back, are a square dovetail frame and two wooden self-supporting stands holding hoop/ring frames; and at the back of the picture is a slate frame supported on trestles.

WORKING WITH HOOPS AND RING FRAMES

BINDING HOOPS

Hoops and ring frames are bound for two reasons – to protect the embroidery fabric from the harshness of the frame and to give a better grip for a tighter tension. Torn strips of calico give a very soft finish, but it is possible to use ready-made bias binding. If possible, bind both hoops, but if not, wrap the outer one only.

To make the strips:

1 Snip the calico on the selvedge and tear off a narrow strip to give a soft edge to the fabric. Snip approximately 2.5cm (1in) along from the edge and tear again to form a long, thin strip.

2 Now begin to wrap it around the outer hoop as this will protect the right side of the embroidery fabric. Wrap the strip around the hoop as if you were putting on a bandage. Try to overlap each wrapping by only half its width, otherwise it will become too bulky and it may not be possible to fit the fabric between the rings. Depending upon the size of the hoop, extra strips may need to be added to complete the binding.

3 Secure both ends with cross stitches and trim off the spare fabric.

WORKING THROUGH A HOLE (CUT AND REVEAL)

This is a good way to use up small, left-over pieces and therefore reduce wastage of expensive fabrics.

1 Cut a square of calico to fit the chosen frame, with a 5cm (2in) seam allowance all round. Loosely mount it into a frame.

2 Draw a square in the centre of the calico 2.5cm (1in) smaller than the piece of background fabric.

3 Either put the fabric on top of the calico (**A**) or place it behind it (**B**). Pin it in place and stitch the two fabrics together with a mixture of quite small running and backstitches to produce a firm join. If placing the fabric behind the calico, it is better to stitch it from the wrong side as it is easy to slip off the unseen edge of the fabric.

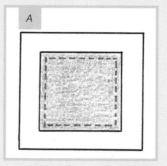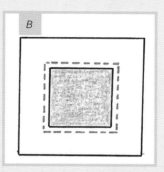

4 Once the fabric is applied to the calico, the window can be carefully cut out. Never cut the window out first, as this produces a distorted shape and will affect the tension.

5 Carefully pull the calico and tighten the frame to create a drum-like tension on the fabric.

If the calico is on top, the fourth side of the cut-out can be left uncut so that the calico forms a flap. This can be used to cover the embroidery when it is not being worked. If the calico is behind, cut the whole square out and keep it. The piece of calico can be used again if the hole is patched. Either fold the flap back and overcast the three sides, or place the cut-out square back in the centre and reattach with large overcasting stitches.

Transferring a design

There are several ways to transfer designs onto fabrics. The method chosen can depend on the fabric being used, the design and personal preference.

Example illustrating trace and tack (see opposite).

TRACING OVER A LIGHT SOURCE

This technique works very well with light-coloured fabrics. Generally, once the design is traced onto the fabric the marks are permanent and the stitchery needs to follow the drawn lines. It is a relatively quick method and will work for any density of design. Note that it is easier to frame up after the design has been traced onto the fabric.

1 Put the design onto the light source. This could be a window, a light box or even a glass coffee table with a desk lamp underneath. Carefully tape the design in place.

2 Lay the fabric over the design, paying attention to the direction of the fabric grain. Firmly tape this in place using a low-tack tape.

3 Trace the design onto the fabric using a marker. The one you choose depends on the fabric, the design and the purpose of the embroidery (see the box, below).

MARKERS

Pencil: 2H and 4H are the most frequently used and the most reliable, as they tend not to smudge or leave any residue. They leave a very light mark that can be removed almost completely with a fabric eraser. This is one of the only methods that is guaranteed not to bleed, rot or damage the fabric and threads, so is ideal for church work and heirlooms. Other useful markers are listed below, but their long-term effects are less well known. They are useful, however, for small projects.

White chalk marker: there are many different chalk markers available and most of them allow the markings to be removed easily.

Permanent marker: as the name suggests, all markings are permanent and need to be covered with stitchery.

Gel pen: makes a permanent mark that needs to be covered. Some are heat-erasable.

Water-erasable pen: usually blue in colour. Before using, check whether removing the colour causes a water mark.

Air-soluble marker: usually blue, white or purple in colour. These markers normally last for one or two days, but can disappear more quickly or stay longer. A residue can be left behind so it is best to cover all the markings.

Paint: oil or acrylic paint can be used but a steady hand is needed to create fine design lines.

TRACE AND TACK

Trace and tack is a very useful method if the working of the design is still uncertain and there is a need for flexibility. It is a time-consuming technique and does not work well with small, intricate designs as the tacking/basting stitches become very confusing, but it can be used with light or dark fabrics. Use a very pale or light-coloured thread for the tacking/basting as this reduces the chance of any noticeable residue being left behind. The fabric needs to be framed up for this technique.

1 Trace the design onto white tissue paper. Use a hard pencil (2H) as this reduces the chance of the tacking/basting thread picking up any residue and marking the fabric.

2 Lay the tracing over the fabric, paying attention to the fabric grain. Carefully hold it in place with a few pins.

3 Tack/baste along the design lines starting from the middle and working outwards. Work a combination of straight stitches with the occasional backstitch. Keep the stitches fairly small.

4 Carefully remove the tissue paper. This can be done in its entirety, or just remove the tissue from the area that is to be worked. The fabric can be protected by leaving some paper in place. Running the point of the needle along the tacking/basting stitches helps to break up the paper for easier removal.

5 When working the embroidery, remove a few tacking/basting stitches at a time.

PRICK AND POUNCE

This is a very old technique that gives an accurate copy of the design on the fabric. It is perfect for dark fabrics that are hard to see through and works best on those that are fairly smooth. It is a clear and relatively quick method and is especially useful if the design needs to be repeated, as the pricking can be re-used again and again. It is possible to pounce with white chalk powder, black charcoal powder or a grey mixture of the two. The black and the grey can be quite messy and become ingrained into the fabric, so they are not used very often. Any excess white chalk brushes off very easily, making it ideal for use on dark, regal-coloured fabrics.

1 Trace the design onto strong tracing paper. Lay the tracing over a foam board, cork mat or other soft surface. Punch holes with a pricker, spacing them a tiny distance (about 1mm) apart all around the design. Lay the pricking over the fabric, paying attention to the fabric grain. The smooth side should be uppermost otherwise the holes will close up when pounced.

2 Rub the pounce through the holes using a pouncer (see page 8), working in a rotating motion. Do not overload the pouncer as the image will become messy and unclear underneath. Carefully remove the tracing. If there is some excess pounce on the fabric, gently blow it away to reveal the design.

3 Join up the dots using a marker. Work from the bottom upwards so as not to smudge the design. Any of the markers listed opposite could be used, depending upon the fabric chosen. Originally, oil paint was used, but this takes a while to dry and can be messy. Acrylic paint is an alternative, but again it is difficult to paint fine lines. Once dry, blow or gently brush away the excess powder.

Padding

Padding can be achieved in a number of different ways to provide a raised area and overall depth to your finished piece of work. Time and care should be taken when attaching the padding as it forms the foundation to your work and has a real impact. Padding is normally completed before any actual embroidery is worked.

SATIN STITCH PADDING

This is worked in embroidery thread and gives a gentle rise to your finished work. It is easy to do, however suitable only for use in small areas covered by satin stitch.

HOW TO WORK SATIN STITCH PADDING

To achieve this raised effect, rows of satin stitch are worked over each other in gradually increasing size to fill the shape and reach the required height. Each row is worked in sequence – horizontally then vertically – with the last row going the opposite way to your finished embroidery. For an example, see the diagram, right. The first row is small and worked one way, for example vertically (**A**). The second row is larger and covers the first and is worked in the opposite way, horizontally (**B**). The next row is larger still and covers the previous row, worked vertically again (**C**). The final embroidery will cover all previous stitching and is worked horizontally (**D**). A domed raised effect is achieved in this way.

FELT PADDING

Felt is a soft material made from fused fibres. Shapes can be cut from it and applied to the background fabric, creating a smooth platform that can be decorated with almost any goldwork technique. It is the best form of padding to use when large areas of a design need to be raised, though any fine, narrow points tend to disintegrate.

HOW TO APPLY FELT

Usually, the colour of the felt used should tone with the colour of the thread being used, as tiny areas may show through once the embroidery is complete and this makes them less visible. Several layers can be attached for added height, but it must be remembered that all these layers will need to be stitched through with most techniques. Attaching kid is one exception, as the leather generally lays over all the padding and only needs to be stitched around the edge.

1 Begin by dividing the area to be padded into layers, similar to the contours on a map. Cut these shapes out of paper and lay them onto the felt, either by holding them down with low-tack tape or drawing around them. Cut them out and start by attaching the smallest piece.

2 Sew down the felt with small straight stitches, coming up in the background fabric and going down into the felt with the needle at a 45-degree angle. Stabilize the felt by placing a stitch in the four main points first (i.e. north, south, east and west) before completing the areas in between with a series of stitches that are approximately 3mm (⅛in) apart. Large pieces may require a second or even third round of preliminary stitches before commencing with the rest. Repeat with all the remaining layers, finishing with the largest (see the photograph bottom right).

Sometimes it is necessary to attach the felt in the reverse order, creating a stepped effect. The example here shows layers of white and yellow for clarity; normally the same colour would be used for each layer.

BUMP AND SOFT COTTON PADDING

Bump is a yellow, softly spun, thick thread that is similar to soft embroidery cotton. If using soft cotton, other colours can also be purchased to blend in with the covering embroidery. Bump and soft cotton fuse well together when couched into a bundle. It is possible to pad narrow areas; alternatively, the whole area can be covered entirely with bump.

It is possible to pad intricate points quite successfully with bump as the padding comprises many separate strands that can be gradually tapered off into a confined space. This provides a firm base when couched down in bundles, or a slightly softer finish if all the strands are stitched down in one go. Whichever version you choose, it is best to use bump for goldwork or silk shading techniques that lay across the padding as it does not have a smooth or sufficiently strong surface to support dense, intrusive embroidery. It is used to pad areas where the metals are attached at the edge of the design, such as kid, cutwork or plate stitched in a zigzag formation.

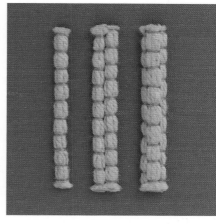

The bundle method of applying bump or soft cotton.

HOW TO APPLY BUMP AND SOFT COTTON PADDING

There are a few methods, but I prefer to use the bundle method. With this method, bundles are stitched down side by side for the first row then more bundles are placed on top, each one straddling two bundles evenly. This is repeated until there is a single bundle on the top; the padding should have a triangular profile, like a pile of logs.

1 Gather four long lengths of bump together. Lay them over the area to be padded and couch down all four pieces into a bundle, spacing the stitches about 3mm (⅛in) apart. If the shape tapers off it is usually easiest to start in the middle of the bundle and work outwards in each direction. None of the bump passes through to the wrong side as it is cleanly cut off at each end; cut the lower pieces first to keep the surface as smooth as possible.

2 Continue couching down the first row of bump, cutting more lengths and laying the bundles side by side until the desired height and shape are achieved.

3 Work the second and subsequent rows in the same way, each bundle straddling two lower bundles each time, until there is just a single bundle at the top.

To lower the height and create shape, gradually taper off by cutting one or two pieces of bump from the bottom of the bundle. This keeps the top surface as smooth as possible.

STRING

String gives a very firm and even base for several goldwork and silk shading techniques. It can be either laid in single pieces or stitched down over an area leaving a string-width in between each length. Household string can be used straight off the ball, though it can be dyed to soften the colour if desired. A light coating of beeswax will hold the fibres together if needed. Many different metals can be stitched across single pieces of string, including broad, 11's and whipped plate, and cutwork using purls.

Methods 1 (top) and 2 (below) for applying string padding.

HOW TO APPLY STRING

String can be attached in a variety of ways, two of which are given below:

1 Start with a straight stitch that goes right over the string then work two further stitches, one from each side of the string, each time taking the needle down into the string. Repeat the pattern of these three stitches all the way along the length, finishing with a stitch that goes across the string. This method holds the string more firmly than the other method (method 1, see right).

2 Hold the string down with a diagonal stitch that runs in the same direction as the twist in the string. Start and finish with a straight stitch (method 2, see right).

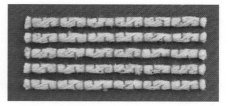

To pad a large area, attach the string leaving a string-width in between each. This allows metals to 'hop' over the lengths and be stitched down in the gaps to create a basketweave effect.

APPLIQUÉ

Appliqué is used to create solid areas of colour by applying cut pieces of fabric to the background. Traditionally, the grain lines of each piece of fabric matched (this was to strengthen the piece) and the fibre content was kept the same, for example silk applied to silk. However, contemporary techniques make use of the different effects that can be created, especially when using shot silk or interesting fabrics, by cutting the shapes out with contrasting grain lines to produce a play of light.

It is best to back any fabric that is going to be applied with a fusible web, such as Bondaweb. This is a fine film of fusible glue with a paper backing and it will bond to a fabric when it is ironed, stopping the edges from fraying too badly. The iron should be heated to a temperature suitable for the fabric being used: medium for silk dupion and low for synthetic fabrics.

HOW TO USE FUSIBLE WEB

Fusible web has a paper backing that can be drawn on. You need to remember to trace off a reversed image, as the fabric will be turned over when it is applied.

1 Lay a piece of fusible web that is bigger than the image over the (reversed) design with the paper uppermost. Trace the design onto the fusible web with a pencil.

2 Iron the piece of fusible web onto the appliqué fabric. Allow this to cool down, then carefully cut out the design following the pencil lines.

3 Peel off the paper backing. Turn the appliqué over and place it in position, sticky side down, on the background fabric. If you wish, place a covering cloth over the appliqué and gently iron it in place.

4 Place straight stitches radiating around the edge of the appliqué to secure it to the fabric (see the diagram right). Use the same method as that for attaching felt (see page 20). Use an invisible or matching thread unless you wish to create a contrasting effect. Make sure that the stitches are neat as they may not be completely covered by the edging.

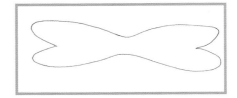

Original image.

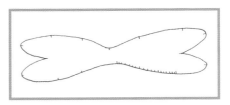

Reversed image.

Securing the appliqué shape with stitches.

The dragonfly wings were created using two layers of green and gold shot organza applied to the background fabric using the method described above. They were then edged with green and gold milliary. See pages 154–155 for this project.

22

Mounting your work

HERRINGBONE METHOD

This method is best worked with a curved needle and a strong, buttonhole-type thread. It works well for larger embroideries.

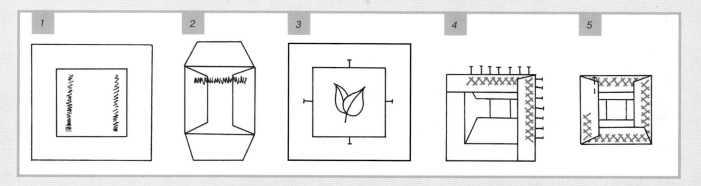

1 Measure the design and work out the desired finished size. Using a piece of foam board, acid-free mount board or grey board, cut a backing board to those dimensions. A thin piece of wadding/batting may be put on the board to give support to the work.

2 Cut a piece of calico approximately 8cm (3in) larger all round than the board. Place the board centrally onto the calico and place a line of glue about 2.5cm (1in) in from the edge of the board on two opposite sides. Leaving this channel makes it easier to stitch down the embroidered piece later on. Press the calico onto the card, pulling the calico taut. Trim all the corners and finally glue the other two side edges.

3 Find the centre of each side of the embroidery and each side of the board. Place the embroidery over the right side of the covered board, and put a pin in each of the centre points.

4 Carefully pin the work to the board, starting from the middle and working outwards. Continue in this manner for the remaining sides. Turn the board over and herringbone stitch the work to the calico, taking care to pull the fabric taut all the time.

5 Mitre or fold each corner as it is reached, making it as flat as possible, but do not cut off the corners of the embroidery.

LACING METHOD

This method can be stitched with either a curved or a large crewel needle using a strong buttonhole thread or crochet cotton. It is best used on small pieces of work otherwise the card tends to buckle.

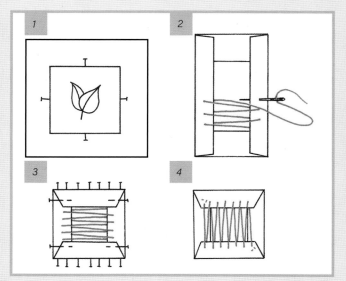

1 Cut the board as in step 1 of the herringbone method and add a thin piece of wadding/batting if desired. Pin the embroidery centrally over the board with four pins then, starting from the middle and working out, pin all around the edges. Trim back the spare edge fabric if necessary but do not cut across any of the corners of the embroidery.

2 Take an extremely long length of thread (about 2m or 80in) and fasten it onto the fabric. Lace two opposite raw edges together. It is best to start with the longest sides first as the shorter stitches will help to hold them down. Loosely lace up the sides, then pull up each thread individually in order to create a taut finish.

3 Fold over the two remaining fabric edges and fold or mitre the corners and pin in place.

4 Lace down the second sides

GOLDWORK

Goldwork embroidery can be found throughout history. It originated in the Far East and travelled west with the silk caravans. It was a symbol of wealth and was used to embellish clothes, homes and religious vestments. Today, goldwork embroidery is still used for ecclesiastical work, the fashion industry and as decoration in homes. It is a specialized form of embroidery with both unique threads and techniques. The threads are relatively expensive but have become more accessible. Threads that contain gold are the most expensive but other metal threads have become available, in which there is no gold at all. It may therefore be more accurate to call it metal thread embroidery.

Goldwork remains, however, a relatively exclusive occupation, as the metals are specially made and only stocked by specialists. The threads come in a wide variety of sizes, weights, metals and colours. The large choice of threads makes it an inspiring form of embroidery, which is constantly evolving, limited only by one's imagination.

RULES FOR GOLDWORK

1 Generally, goldwork is best worked from the foreground going backwards. This is because most of the metals are quite firm and do not overlay each other easily. A strong, smooth shape is thus created first and then everything else slots up to it. If you try it from the background to foreground you can end up with some interesting and distorted shapes.

2 Use short lengths of sewing thread, up to 45cm (18in), to prevent threads shredding or becoming tangled.

3 Coat polyester or silk threads with beeswax to strengthen and smooth them. Use these threads for hidden stitchery and/or decorative areas. The metal threads will shred them if they are not strengthened.

4 Be careful not to over-handle metal threads, especially if they are silver plate or 90 per cent silver. The acidity in your fingers can lead to the thread tarnishing and turning grey or even black.

5 Goldwork is very tactile and tempting to touch, but this should be avoided as touching the threads too often can damage them, denting them and changing their appearance.

6 Goldwork threads are expensive, so try not to waste them when leaving ends to plunge – generally leave 2.5cm (1in). This is enough to take through the fabric without too much difficulty, but not an excessive length to add to the overall amount needed.

7 Cover your work when you have a break from your embroidery. This stops unwanted things landing on your work. A shower cap (see above, right) is ideal for most ring frames; you could use a piece of fabric or even a clean tea towel for larger embroideries. A good idea, especially if working on a pale background, is to 'work through a hole'. This can be a piece of calico with a 10cm (4in) square or circle cut into it. You lay this across the fabric so that the hole is positioned over the area you are working on. It can then be moved from section to section, exposing just the area you need, but protecting the remaining fabric. (See bottom image on page 17.)

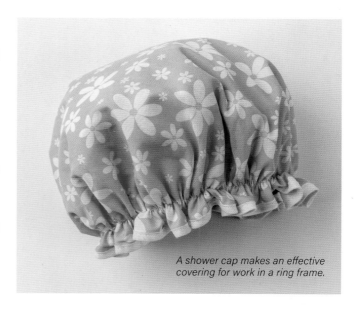

A shower cap makes an effective covering for work in a ring frame.

8 Always leave threads that are retained for further stitching on the right side of the work so they do not become tangled underneath. Make sure you do this in an area of the design that will later be covered with embroidery in case the needle or thread leaves a mark.

9 If you are continuing to use the same sewing thread for several processes, always secure the thread in between each in a hidden area.

10 When using purls, only keep a small number on your velvet board, minimizing potential damage or loss.

11 When your work is finished, remember that goldwork does not like excessive heat, damp or direct sunlight, so think carefully where to display or store it.

ORDER OF WORK

Goldwork is stitched from the foreground working towards the background. Stitching complete shapes and gradually working towards the broken areas gives the cleanest lines to the main elements, which the rest then merge with.

There are some general rules that apply when deciding on the order of work, but there are some exceptions. Always take into account the overall design and the techniques you are using. The aim is to produce flowing lines in your work, so pay particular attention to sweeping lines such as stems and veins. It is often best to put these in first, otherwise the lines could become misshapen. Also think about the fragility of some of the metals. Some of the purls are quite soft and easily damaged, so if possible leave high relief work until nearer the end to avoid squashing them. Stem stitch formation (see page 34) is a perfect example of this, as it is quite high relief and fairly soft.

Generally, it is better to work filled shapes by starting with the outline and then infilling with a technique. This contains the embroidery and stops it 'growing' and becoming too chunky. However, some techniques need to be worked first and then embellished, for example kid or fabric appliqué and Elizabethan twist (see page 46).

When considering possible new designs:

- Study the design carefully, dividing it into sections. Start in the foreground and work towards the background.
- Look at any strong lines, such as stems and veins.
- Think about possible techniques that would suit each area and the design as a whole.
- Decide if any padding is to be included.
- Consider if any leather or fabric is to be applied.
- Think about the possibility of introducing a colour.

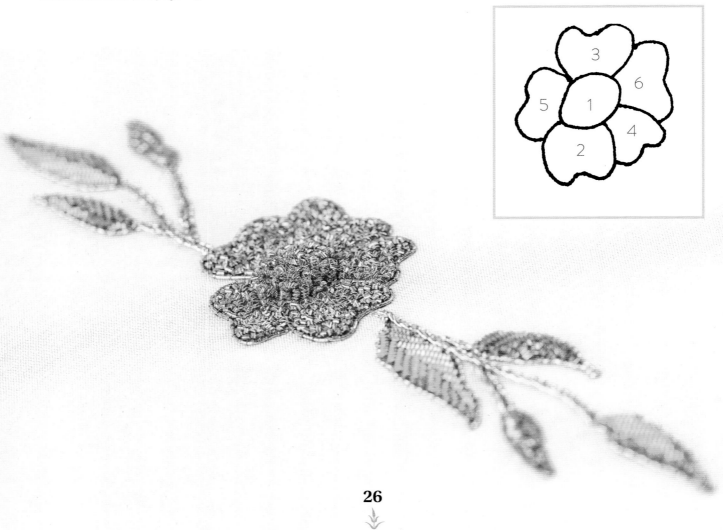

Metal threads

Metal threads can be divided into two main categories: those that are hollow and are attached by passing a sewing thread through them as if stitching on a bead, and couching threads that have a solid core and are held down with stitches across the metal (couched). Below are examples of some of the metal threads but it is not all that are available. Each thread is shown in gold colour, but there are many different coloured threads available.

SEWING THREADS

These are used to attach goldwork threads to the fabric but can also be used decoratively.

Heavy metal thread: a very fine, metallic sewing thread available in several colours of gold and silver. This thread knots really easily, so only use short lengths.

Ophir thread: a 3-ply metallic sewing thread available in gold and silver colours.

Cords: fine metallic sewing threads available in a wide range of colours.

In addition to these are fine silk and polyester sewing threads. These need to be waxed before use (see page 8). With all the above threads it is best to match the colour with the colour of the metal being applied. Within each technique section on the following pages, suggestions are given as to which sewing thread could be used.

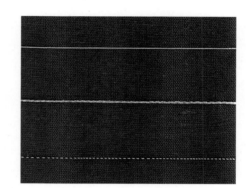

Heavy metal thread

Ophir thread

Cord 205C

Note

All of the thread samples on pages 27–30 have been enlarged by about 50 per cent to aid identification.

HOLLOW THREADS

There are four types of hollow purl: bright check, wire check, smooth and rough. The only real difference between them is their appearance as they can all be treated in the same way. All can be cut into lengths and threaded through as if sewing on a bead. They are usually held down with a single length of waxed polyester or silk thread, but sometimes it is necessary to use a metallic sewing thread (heavy metal thread) to disguise the stitches.

Sizes of purl range from no. 10 (finest) to no. 4 (largest) for 2 per cent gold, gilt, 90 per cent silver, silver plate and copper, with the most popular sizes being no. 6 and no. 8. Coloured purls are also available.

HANDLING PURLS

Be careful with all the purls as they are fragile. If any fall down onto the carpet, do not just pick them up. Very carefully find the ends and slowly lift these first, checking that none of the metal has attached itself to the carpet. Once any of the purls have become stretched and distorted they will never resume their original shape. Always work with purls on a velvet board (see page 8), which provides a firm and stable base for them. Only keep a small amount out at a time on the velvet board to minimize any damage should you accidentally spill them.

CUTTING PURLS

All these hollow purls are best cut on a velvet board. Sometimes pieces are cut by eye, and other times they need to be measured accurately. The easiest way to cut purls is to lay them on the board and snip them with the tips of the scissors. Use the velvet board like an artist's palette, to contain small, separate piles of different types of chipping (see pages 31–32 for more on chippings).

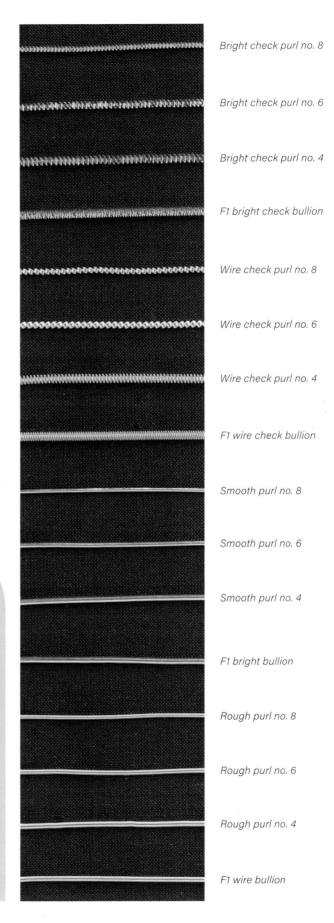

Bright check purl no. 8

Bright check purl no. 6

Bright check purl no. 4

F1 bright check bullion

Wire check purl no. 8

Wire check purl no. 6

Wire check purl no. 4

F1 wire check bullion

Smooth purl no. 8

Smooth purl no. 6

Smooth purl no. 4

F1 bright bullion

Rough purl no. 8

Rough purl no. 6

Rough purl no. 4

F1 wire bullion

COUCHED THREADS

Couching threads are made by wrapping a metallic strip or thread around a fibre core. This makes the cut ends fragile and they can unravel easily, so a tail needs to be left at the start and finish of each row, which is plunged through to the back of the work and fastened off securely behind the stitchery.

Japs (Japanese threads): round threads with a very bright, smooth appearance.

T numbers (imitation Japs): round threads with a softly toned finish.

Passing: a very flexible, round, fine thread that is available in a smooth or wavy finish.

Check thread and 8 x 2 check thread: both are round threads with a closer, zigzag appearance.

Rococco: a round thread with a soft, long, undulating appearance.

Flatworm: a rounded thread with a flattened appearance.

Elizabethan twist: a very fine, 2-ply twist.

PEARL PURLS

Pearl purl is a stiff, domed wire that is tightly coiled to create a long firm thread that is easy to shape and cut to length. When couched down it looks like tiny beads sitting next to each other.

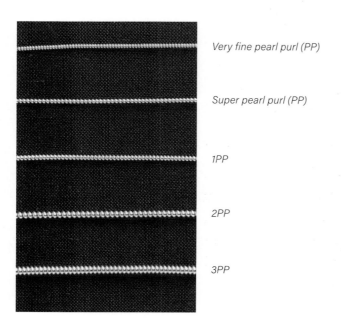

Very fine pearl purl (PP)

Super pearl purl (PP)

1PP

2PP

3PP

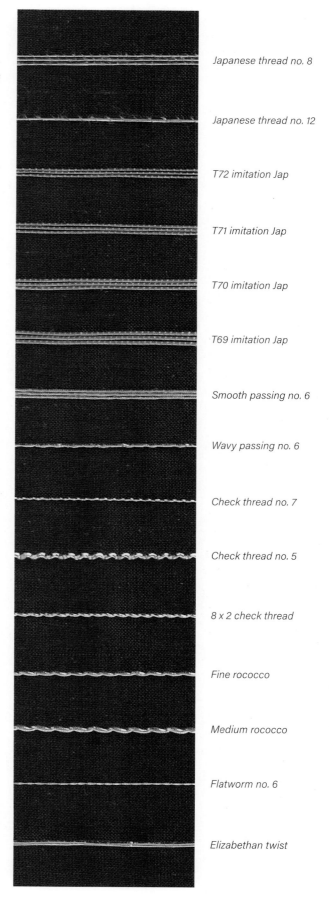

Japanese thread no. 8

Japanese thread no. 12

T72 imitation Jap

T71 imitation Jap

T70 imitation Jap

T69 imitation Jap

Smooth passing no. 6

Wavy passing no. 6

Check thread no. 7

Check thread no. 5

8 x 2 check thread

Fine rococco

Medium rococco

Flatworm no. 6

Elizabethan twist

TWISTS

Twists are made by plying several couching threads together. Like couching threads, therefore, the cut ends are fragile and can unravel easily, so a tail needs to be left at the start and finish of each row that is later plunged through to the back of the work and fastened off securely. There are numerous varieties available.

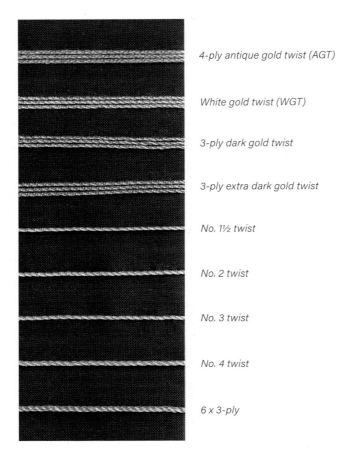

4-ply antique gold twist (AGT)

White gold twist (WGT)

3-ply dark gold twist

3-ply extra dark gold twist

No. 1½ twist

No. 2 twist

No. 3 twist

No. 4 twist

6 x 3-ply

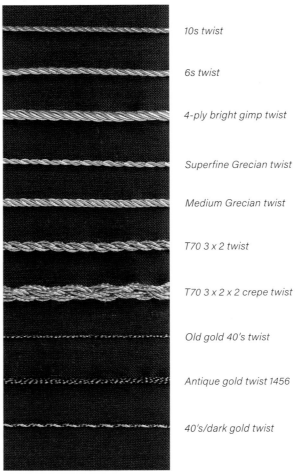

10s twist

6s twist

4-ply bright gimp twist

Superfine Grecian twist

Medium Grecian twist

T70 3 x 2 twist

T70 3 x 2 x 2 crepe twist

Old gold 40's twist

Antique gold twist 1456

40's/dark gold twist

Goldwork techniques

PURL CHIPPINGS

Purl chippings are tiny pieces of purl, usually bright check or wire check, that are sewn down in a random yet organized way. Also referred to as seeding, this is a very useful technique for filling small, awkwardly shaped spaces. Any of the hollow purls – rough, smooth, wire check or bright check – are cut up into tiny pieces approximately 1–2mm (1/16in) in size by snipping them on a velvet board. Traditionally, the chippings are cut square, in which the length equals the width, as this allows the area to be filled more compactly. Occasionally, exceptionally small pieces are required to complete any tiny gaps.

The chippings are generally sewn down with a single waxed polyester thread in a colour that matches the metal being used, for example muted yellow to attach gold or white to apply silver. However, when using very fine purls, it is easier to pass a heavy metal thread through the tiny eye of the no. 10 sharps needle that is required. Whichever thread is chosen it must be used throughout the entire piece of work to achieve a consistent look.

Chippings are usually sewn down in random directions so that the little pieces of purl (particularly bright check and wire check) sparkle as they catch the light. Ensuring the chippings are truly haphazard, so that the spirals do not lie in the same direction, requires some thought. The chippings must also lie adjacent to each other without overlapping, and it is important to make the stitches the same length as the piece of metal being attached otherwise the chippings will not lie flat against the fabric (see the diagram, right). More textural effects can be made by mixing different purls together to create 'purl soup', or by altering the lengths and experimenting with the direction and spacing of the chippings.

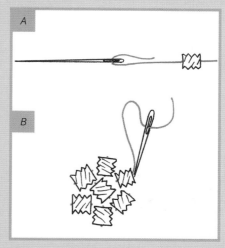

The best way to attach chippings is to thread on a length of purl and push it all the way down the attaching thread (A) to the surface of the fabric. Lay the purl down against the fabric in the desired direction and take the needle down at the end of the purl (B). Continue in the same way, constantly changing direction until the area is completely filled.

Spaced chippings of bright check purl no. 6.

Traditionally spaced chippings of wire check purl no. 6.

Long, openly spaced chippings of smooth purl no. 6.

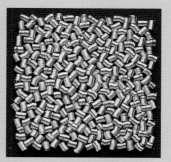

Short, closely stitched pieces of rough purl no. 4.

Gradually dispersed chippings of bright check purl no. 6 from dense to openly spaced.

Bright check purl, graded in size from the bottom left-hand corner to the top right, large to fine (nos. 4, 6 and 8).

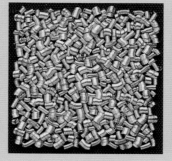

A random mix of different sizes of rough purl, nos. 4 and 8.

Purl soup. A variety of sizes and types of purl sewn down in a random mixture.

SHADING WITH CHIPPINGS

You can create beautiful shaded effects by changing the colour of the chippings throughout a design.

Begin by making a drawing of your design. Look carefully at the drawing and divide it into separate parts. Try to include at least three colours that tone or look good together. They need to grade through in order within a shape, and where one shape needs to stand away from another, two contrasting colours should be used where the two shapes overlap.

It is best to stitch one shape at a time, working from the foreground backwards. This allows you to adapt the design where necessary, altering the shading to make certain areas stand out. To help blend the colours together, try to make the joins as feathery as possible to help lead the eye through the colour change. Achieve this by working the last row of one colour with gaps left in it so that they can be filled with the next colour.

The violet flowers are worked in shaded chips of silver, lavender and violet purl. These shades were chosen to produce a natural effect. They highlight the light hitting the petals and areas of shade, giving depth and beauty to the flowers (see pages 52–53 for this project).

FUZZY EFFECT

This is a modern technique using purls that have been distorted. It can be used to form a highly textured area and covers a relatively large area quickly. The thread can be tightly packed to form a dense area or teased apart to form a lighter, more delicate effect. It is also possible to shade using this method by teasing the different colours together when tying them down. The thread used for tying them down is generally heavy metal in the matching colour, or invisible thread so it cannot be seen.

To achieve this effect, cut a length of purl roughly 2.5cm (1in) long. Stretch it until it is almost straight, leaving a slight kink in the length. Fold the extended length in half and repeat four times. Roll the folded thread in the palms of your hands until it forms a ball shape. Place this in the desired area and tease and couch it into position, pulling the purl apart until you get the required covering.

Continue in this way, adding to the first piece so all new sections are teased together seamlessly, working outwards from the centre. All the leaves on the bonsai tree, shown right and on pages 106–107, are worked in this way to provide the delicate shaded and textured effect required.

GRADED CUTWORK

Hollow purls can be carefully cut to fit a shape exactly, resembling satin stitch – a technique known as graded cutwork. This is a good technique for smooth, flowing shapes. Think of the metal threads as flexible beads and sew them down by pushing the thread up the length of the purl, just as you would with a bugle bead. Generally, cut lengths of purl are attached with a single waxed polyester thread in a colour that matches the metal. Occasionally, it is necessary to use a heavy metal thread, as this is easier to thread through the finer sharps and straw needles when stitching down very fine purls.

Graded cutwork can be worked flat onto the background fabric, but it is easier to work over padding (bump, felt, string or carpet felt). Often it is helpful to start the cutwork from the centre of the area to be stitched, in which case mark a centre line on the fabric to follow. This makes it easier to maintain the same angle all the way down the shape. A good diagonal to work with is 45 degrees to the design line, but this can alter depending upon the curve of the motif.

1 It is advisable to outline the shape first, although it is possible to edge it afterwards. Pearl purl or a check thread is ideal for this purpose. It creates a boundary within which to work the cutwork, and it stops the shape from spreading, keeping it neat and contained.

2 Bring the needle out at a 45-degree angle next to the goldwork edge. Lay the chosen purl over the shape and carefully cut it to fit. Do this by either denting the purl with your fingernail and cutting away from the work, or cutting it directly with fine-pointed scissors.

3 Thread the cut length of purl onto the sewing thread and take the needle down next to the edge on the other side of the shape. Work in a backstitch motion to help the purls lie tidily across the fabric. Continue all the way up the shape, keeping an eye on the angle.

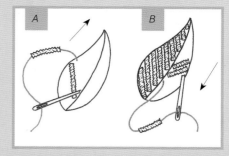

Work the cutwork in a backstitch motion: (A) working upwards and (B) working downwards. In (A), bring the needle out on the edge and take it down on the centre line; in (B), bring the needle out on the centre line and take it down on the edge of the leaf. This way of working produces a longer and stronger stitch on the back of the work.

CUTTING LENGTHS OF PURL

Cutting the lengths of purl to the correct size is quite hard to do and the purl may need to be taken off the needle and adjusted several times. It is worth taking your time with this to create a smooth satin stitch effect. If the purl length is too short the sewing thread will be revealed, and if it is too long it will stand proud of the fabric like a bridge. Cut each length so that it lays across the fabric comfortably between the boundary lines.

Opposite: see pages 106–107 for details on stitching this piece.

Right: graded cutwork over string and bump; for the full piece, see pages 96–97.

STEM STITCH FORMATION

Pieces of purl can be cut into lengths and sewn down in a stem stitch formation, a process sometimes referred to as s-ing. Stem stitch formation can be used either in the form of a solitary line or in conjunction with other metals. It gives height and texture to a design but is fairly fragile, so apply it as late as possible to reduce the risk of damage.

The needle always comes out on the same side of the design line, producing a rope-like effect. Stem stitch formation can be made from any of the hollow purls – rough, smooth, bright check and wire check, though the twisted effect shows up best with the straight purls (rough and smooth) or when combining a straight purl with a faceted one (for example, rough with bright check purl). It is usually worked with a single waxed polyester thread.

It is important to cut the purl as accurately as possible using a ruler and velvet board (see page 8): just over 6mm (¼in) is a good measurement for no. 6 purls and 5mm (just over ³⁄₁₆in) works well for finer no. 8 purls, though other sizes can be cut depending upon the degree of twist required and the thickness of the metal. Generally, short pieces of purl make tighter spiralling twists.

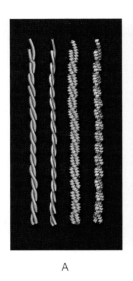    

A	B	C	D	E

Each of the samples on the left shows a square finish at the bottom of each row where an extra half length has been added, and a tapered finish at the top. All the samples were cut to just over 6mm (¼in) lengths.

(A) four types of purl – rough, smooth, wire check and bright check no. 6;

(B) alternating purls – rough and bright check no. 6;

(C) alternating thicknesses using rough purl no. 6 and wire check no. 4;

(D) chevron effect using two rows of rough purl no. 6 with one reversed;

(E) combining stem stitch with pairs of couched smooth passing no. 6.

CREATING STEM STITCH FORMATION

This is the easiest way of creating a smooth finish as it follows the traditional way of creating stem stitch in embroidery.

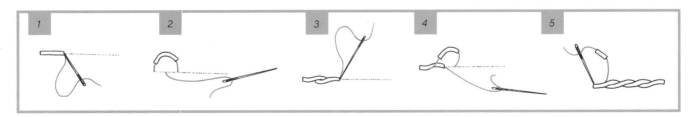

1 Cut the purl into identical lengths of your chosen size with the aid of a ruler on a velvet board. Fasten a thread on the design line and come out in the desired place. Thread on one of the cut lengths of purl and gently push it down the thread as far as it will go without damaging it. Lay the piece of purl flat against the fabric and take the needle down at the end of the purl.

2 Pull the thread through to the wrong side, leaving it slack on the front. Bring the needle up halfway between the two threads and pull the thread up, as shown.

3 Thread on a new piece of purl and push it down as far as it will go. Take the needle down at the end of the second piece of purl.

4 Pull it through, but again leave it loose, as it is easier to see where to bring the needle up if the purl is out of the way. Bring the needle up halfway between the two threads, as before.

5 Continue like this until the desired length is achieved. Half pieces can be added to either end of the line to create a squarer finish.

PURL LOOPS

These can be made from any of the hollow purls – bright check, wire check, rough or smooth purl. They are cut to accurate lengths using a ruler on a velvet board and generally attached with a matching waxed polyester thread, but sometimes it is useful to use heavy metal thread, as any surface stitches will become invisible. Different effects can be achieved by altering the type of purl used and how it is attached to the fabric – it can be stitched down as a single loop or as continuous loops, held against the fabric or freestanding.

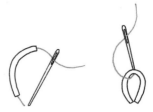

Forming a single loop.

SINGLE LOOP

This looks like a detached chain stitch; 12mm (½in) lengths of purl are a good size to work with. Bring the needle out through the fabric and thread on a purl. Take the needle back down into almost the same hole and gently pull it up. The loop or chain stitch can be held down with a stitch across the top of the arc or it can be left freestanding; it can be left as it is or decorated with other pieces of purl. Loops can even be placed inside loops to create a solid filling. The purl can be deliberately stretched so that when it is sewn down the attaching stitches show through. Red stitches, for example, could be used to add colour to the gold. Flower patterns can be made by arranging the purl loops around a stone or purl.

Decorating single loops.

ARCHES OR SCALES

These are multiple single loops that are attached by bringing the needle out through the fabric, threading on a length of purl and going back down some distance away from the starting point. Hold the top of the arch down with a single stitch placed over the purl. Build up a series of these open-ended loops and either leave them plain or fill them with chippings or even smaller loops.

Arches or scales.

CHAIN STITCH

This is a continuous line of loops. Make a single loop or chain stitch and bring the needle back up inside the arc. Thread on another piece of purl and go down inside the arc of the first stitch, pulling up the thread. Continue like this until the desired length is achieved and finish the line with a stitch taken over the arc. Take care with continuous chains as it is very easy for a stitch to slip out of the previous loop and break the chain.

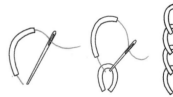

Chain stitch.

MAGIC OR CHEQUERED CHAIN

This is the same as chain stitch but the type of purl used is alternated along the line.

Magic or chequered chain.

ZIGZAG CHAIN

This is the same as chain stitch except that the loops or chains are positioned at angles to each other.

Zigzag chain.

CHAIN WITH PURL DECORATION

Work a row of chain stitch in rough or smooth purl and then embellish it with lengths of a contrasting purl such as bright or wire check purl.

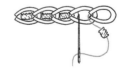

Chain with purl decoration.

CABLE CHAIN

Chains are linked together with lengths of purl. Cut no. 8 rough or smooth purl into 12mm (½in) pieces and cut no. 8 bright or wire check purl into 5mm (³⁄₁₆in) pieces. Sew down a line of single chains first then link them together with the check purl.

Cable chain.

COUCHED THREADS

Couching is the term used for attaching metallic (or other) threads by working stitches over them at regular intervals. It can be used for working single lines, laidwork/lattice patterns and filling large areas. A variety of threads can be used to couch down the metals depending upon whether the stitch is to be visible or disguised. For example, the attaching thread could be a waxed polyester thread that either tones with the metal or contrasts with it, or a matching metallic thread, like heavy metal thread, that will blend in.

When choosing a couching thread, consider the technique being used (straight lines, curves or multiple rows, with or without turns) and the effect required (bright, muted or textured). Japs, T numbers and smooth passing are the most popular threads, but other types could also be used. Passing and T numbers are very flexible, producing neat turns. They therefore work well with Or Nué with turned edges and over string for a basketweave effect. Japs are created from a much broader strip of metal wrapped around a core, making them less pliable and more suited to straight lines and gently curving arcs that do not require turns. Rococco and check threads are useful where an interesting texture is required.

COUCHING DOWN THREADS

Finer threads are frequently couched down two at a time (see diagram below left). In this case, make sure that the couching stitch is as broad as the two pieces of metal being attached otherwise the threads will look pinched in, and keep the threads lying flat side by side. Always leave 2.5cm (1in) ends overhanging the design line that can be plunged later. Space the couching stitches approximately 3–6mm (³⁄₁₆–¼in) apart depending upon the thickness of the thread, and place them at right angles to the design line.

WORKING MULTIPLE ROWS

When working multiple rows, angle the needle at 45 degrees when couching over the second and subsequent rows. This helps to reduce any gaps between the rows as the threads slide closer to each other. Bring the needle up a thread-width away from the existing row and place the needle so that it is pointing towards the stitchery at a 45-degree angle. Using a brick pattern also creates a smoother appearance (see the diagram below right).

To stop the core becoming visible as the metal is couched down, carefully tighten the thread up by twisting it once it has been attached. Make sure that you turn it in the same direction as the plies otherwise it will reveal the core even more. This works only if the couched line is fairly short and the stitchery is not too tight. Twisting the thread also helps to straighten out the line.

There are many types of threads that can be couched:

Straight/smooth threads
Japs/Japanese threads
  (very shiny)
T numbers/imitation Japs
  (muted colours)
Smooth and wavy passing
  (bright colours)

Flat threads
Flatworm (flat and shiny)

Textured wavy threads
Check threads (angular waves)
Rococco (undulating waves)

Twisted threads
Numerous types (these can
  also be attached by stitching
  between the plies)

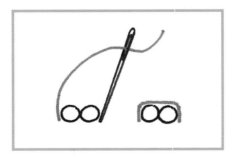

Couching over two threads.

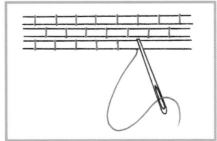

Working multiple rows of couching.

ROWS

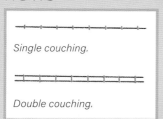

Single couching.

Double couching.

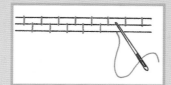

Triple couching, where a third piece is added to a pair of threads and the needle goes down between the first pair of threads.

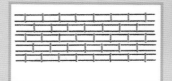

Bricking pairs of threads.

Single rococco.

DIAPER PATTERNS

Many diaper patterns can be achieved with couching. Experiment with single threads and couched pairs. Any geometric pattern can be used, and inspiration can come from other forms of embroidery such as blackwork or by simply looking around at familiar objects like brick patterns, roof tiles or even tyre treads.

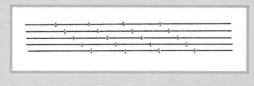

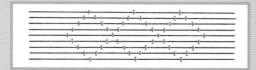

Double rococco couched together.

POINTS

The most accurate and sharpest points are achieved by plunging the ends; on shallow angles, turning is easier. Separate the metal threads at the point, taking a single couching thread over the outer one first, followed by a stabilizing stitch in a hidden area. Then take a stitch over the inner thread and again secure it with a hidden stitch. Now return to attaching the threads in pairs. Occasionally, it is useful to add a holding stitch over the single threads at the point.

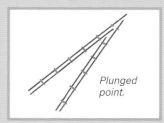

Plunged point.

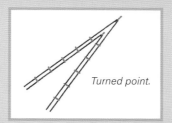

Turned point.

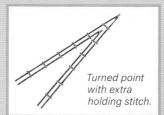

Turned point with extra holding stitch.

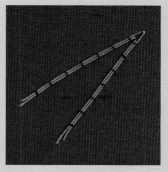

Double, triple and bricked T70.

TURNS

Turning the edges wherever possible is more economical of thread and time, but plunging the ends produces a smoother finish. Generally, if using two threads it is easier to establish the outer edge before dealing with the inner thread. The following diagrams have the lower couching stitches missing so that it is easier to see the turning stitches.

Turned point: paired T70.

Single thread stitched in a brick pattern with turned edges. Two single diagonal stitches are used at each turn.

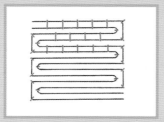

Double threads stitched in a brick pattern with turned edges. Work two single diagonal stitches on the outer thread first, then turn the inner thread with a single horizontal stitch.

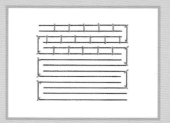

Double threads stitched in a brick pattern with turns and plunged ends. A new thread is added at each turn as the previous thread is plunged.

CONTINUOUS COUCHING

This creates interesting patterns as tiny sections of the background fabric show through. This is even more effective if stitched on a contrasting colour background, for example gold on black. The best shape is achieved by stitching from the outside and working towards the middle.

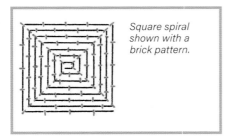

Square spiral shown with a brick pattern.

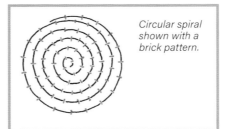

Circular spiral shown with a brick pattern.

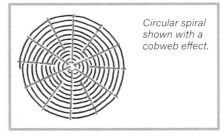

Circular spiral shown with a cobweb effect.

Winter tree
A winter tree showing a number of different couching methods:

Continuous couched passing;

Couched 3-ply twist;

Couched rococco;

and pearl purl.

TWISTS

Twists can be either commercially made or custom-made by hand. They can be attached in several different ways depending on the look you wish to achieve: as single lines, multiple rows or combined with other metals. Twists can be couched down in a running-stitch motion, or they can be more firmly attached using a backstitch motion with the longer stitches on the back of the work. Space the couching stitches between 3mm and 6mm (⅛in and ¼in) apart depending upon the size of the twist. Always leave at least 2.5cm (1in) overhanging the edge of the design at both the starting and finishing points. These ends are then taken down (plunged) through the fabric once all the twist has been attached. It is best to take all parts of the twist through in one go otherwise it can become distorted.

Twists can be plied to spiral in either an 'S' or 'Z' twist direction, so-called because the twist follows the path of the middle part of the letter. This can also apply to threads as they are spun around a core in a particular direction. Different effects can be created by combining twists displaying both angles.

STRAIGHT COUCHING

This method is ideal for very smooth, plain twists where it is hard to see the individual plies. The stitches lie over the twist at right angles to the design line. They can be either blended in with the twist by using a heavy metal thread or deliberately left visible by using a waxed coloured sewing thread.

DIAGONAL COUCHING

This method is best used on a twist that has a visible direction as the stitches follow the roll of the plies. Bring the needle out in line with one of the plies, lay the thread over the twist following the angle and go down into the fabric.

COUCHING BETWEEN THE PLIES

This method attaches the twist to the fabric invisibly as the stitches drop down in between the plies. The stitches can be sewn down in either a backstitch or a running-stitch motion. Bring the needle up through the fabric and take it down in between the threads. If it resists, the needle is probably trying to pierce a ply so remove the needle and try again.

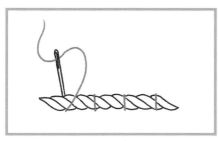

Straight couching.

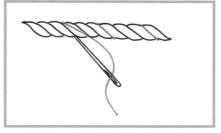

Diagonal couching.

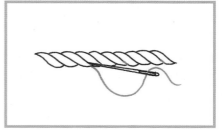

Couching between the plies.

These samples show a selection of commercial 3-ply twists of (from left to right): white gold, sunrise opal, sunset opal, copper, red, claret, purple, navy, blue, cedar, emerald, grass green and white gold. The samples have been enlarged for clarity.

HANDMADE TWISTS

Custom-made twists can be made from a variety of different metallic threads. It is not possible to combine a 'Z' twist with an 'S' twist as the twisting process will unwind one as the other is tightened, so look carefully at the threads to make sure they are compatible before you proceed. If necessary, twist the chosen threads loosely between your fingers to see roughly what the twist will look like. To reduce or enlarge the thickness of the finished twist, adjust the quantities of threads used. Twists can be made from Japs, T numbers, smooth passing, 3-ply twists, check threads, rococco and many other embroidery threads.

Twists can be made with a cord winder (see page 8) or by using pencils. A cord winder generally gives a tighter and firmer twist, but not everyone has access to one. The pencil method is described right.

Shown below are three different types of twist. All are made using the same method, but made varying the types and numbers of threads used and the way they are attached to the pencils.

PENCIL METHOD

This technique is easier with two people. Calculate how much twist is actually required, including allowances for plunging ends and attaching to the pencils. Also add about 20 per cent of the finished length to allow for shrinkage, then double the final figure as the twist will be doubled back on itself.

1 Cut a length of the chosen thread and tie a pencil to each end. Hold a pencil each and stand facing each other, keeping the thread taut and level. Place your thumb and forefinger of the left hand on the thread near the knot and use your right hand to turn the pencil. Make sure that you are both tightening the thread and not undoing it!

2 Twist the threads until they start to kink, then one person carefully takes hold of the centre of the thread while handing their pencil to the other, still keeping a tension on the thread.

3 Slowly release the thread, about 2.5cm (1in) at a time, until the complete length has twisted.

The pencil method of making handmade twists.

PLAIN TWISTS

Using a single type of thread, tie the length or lengths to the pencils, twist and fold them back on themselves.

One length of gold T69 (makes a 1 x 1 twist).

Two lengths of gold T69 (makes a 2 x 2 twist).

Three lengths of gold T69 (makes a 3 x 3 twist).

STRIPED TWIST

Cut lengths of two different threads. Tie them together end to end and tie the remaining ends to the pencils. Twist and fold the threads back on themselves.

Two lengths of gold T69 and two of copper T69.

Twelve lengths of gold T69 and four of copper T69.

Six lengths of copper T70 and six of gold check thread no. 7.

MOTTLED TWIST

Lay two different threads side by side and knot them together at each end. Slip a pencil in at each end, twist and fold.

One length of gold T69 and one length of copper T69.

Three lengths of gold T70 and three lengths of copper T70.

Two lengths of gold T70 and one length of gilt medium rococco.

MILLIARY

Milliary is a delicate-looking, smooth thread with a looped edge that lies flat against the fabric and gives a soft finish to edges. It resembles stretched pearl purl sewn alongside a passing thread and it is best held down with invisible stitches of heavy metal thread, pinning the milliary in place first (see the diagram, right). The usual way of finishing the thread is to cut the ends flush with the edge of the design and couch over them firmly. Alternatively, leave approximately 2.5cm (1in) tails overhanging the design, then carefully unwind the milliary and take the spun threads through to the back of the fabric. The firm spiral component is then cut off to fit the design line (see below). Milliary can be couched as a single line, back to back, facing inwards or in multiple rows to cover an entire area (see also page 42).

Holding the milliary in place with pins before stitching.

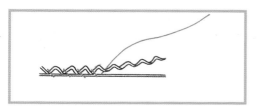

1. Unwind the milliary.

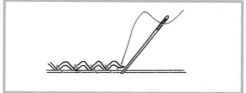

2. Trim off the firm spiral and plunge the other two flexible threads.

SINGLE LINE

There are two ways of attaching milliary as a single line: either bringing the couching thread up through the loops and taking it down over the smooth thread, or vice versa. If it is the first metal to be stitched down, choose the method that you find easier to work. However, if it is be placed next to existing metal threads it is better to come up through the loops and go down over the smooth thread as this pulls the threads closer together.

A single line of milliary can be 'threaded through' with a contrasting thread for a more decorative effect. This is best done before the milliary is applied. Leave 2.5cm (1in) tails on the contrasting thread that can be plunged later.

BACK TO BACK

Lay two pieces of milliary on the fabric with the straight edges touching and pin them in place. Stitch them down together, coming up through the loops on one side and down into the loops on the other. The stitches may wander a little as the spacing of the loops changes slightly along the milliary, so disguise this by using a thread that blends into the metal.

Back-to-back milliary can be embellished by adding an extra metal thread on top. To create a wider band, attach the additional metal after the first piece of milliary but before the second piece.

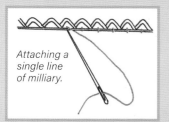

Attaching a single line of milliary.

Threaded-through milliary.

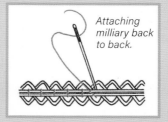

Attaching milliary back to back.

Embellishing back-to-back milliary.

FACING INWARDS

This is simply two single rows sewn with the looped edges facing each other. Facing-inwards milliary can be further embellished by lacing a thread through the loops. This is best done before the milliary is applied. A zigzag effect can be achieved by lacing through alternate loops. Leave 2.5cm (1in) tails on the lacing thread that can be plunged later.

LOOK ALIKE

Two separate rows (one of smooth passing and one of over-stretched pearl purl) are attached to resemble milliary. It does not matter which is applied first, but when stitching down the second metal take an occasional stitch over both pieces. Cut off the spare pearl purl and plunge the tails of the smooth passing.

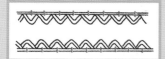

Attaching milliary facing inwards.

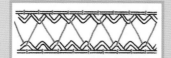

Laced facing-inwards milliary.

Look alike.

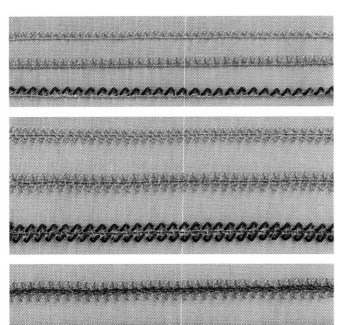

Single line
Traditional milliary (top), large milliary (centre), coloured milliary (bottom).

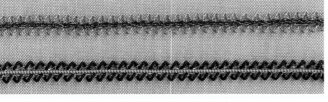

Back to back
Traditional milliary (top), large milliary (centre), coloured milliary (bottom).

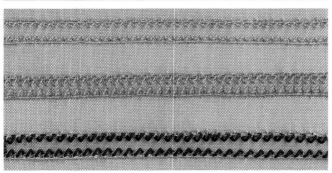

Embellished back to back
Large milliary embellished with royal 3-ply twist (top), coloured milliary embellished with very fine PP (bottom).

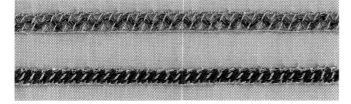

Facing inwards
Traditional milliary (top), large milliary (centre), coloured milliary (bottom).

Laced facing inwards
Large milliary laced with royal 3-ply twist (top), coloured milliary tightly laced with smooth passing no. 6 (bottom).

Threaded through (single line)
Large milliary threaded through with royal 3-ply twist.

Look alike
Stretched 2PP and smooth passing no. 6.

Multiple rows
Large milliary, each row placed in the same direction. Any of the techniques mentioned above can be stitched down in multiple rows to create interesting effects.

Note
All of the samples above are stitched down with heavy metal thread and are enlarged by approximately 75 per cent to aid identification.

PLUNGING THREADS

There are several terms for this technique – sinking, plunging or taking threads through to the wrong side. It is essential to plunge any of the threads that have fibre cores wrapped with a metallic strip as they are fragile at the ends and could fray if simply cut off. It is important to leave 2.5cm (1in) long tails at the start and end of each thread in order to fasten off the thread successfully.

Thinner threads are easier to plunge than thicker ones. Fine imitation Jap, passing and check thread go through the fabric very smoothly; some twists are a little more difficult. It is helpful to use a stiletto, mellore or even a large chenille needle to make a preliminary hole; any of these will gently push the weave of the fabric apart without damaging it. Carefully push the tool into the fabric at the chosen position and wiggle it about. This makes it easier subsequently to pull the needle through the fabric.

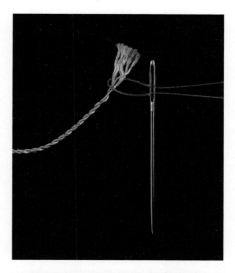

STRIPPING BACK THE THREAD

Before plunging, all threads benefit from having the end stripped back by about 12mm (½in) to reveal the inner core. This allows the needle and thread to pass through the fabric more easily as the stripped end will fold back gently against the complete thread and create less resistance. To strip back a thread, hold it firmly between your thumb and forefinger to avoid stripping back too much and gently pull on the metal thread.

THREADING THE NEEDLE

Thread the stripped end into the needle, stopping where the complete thread starts. It is important to place all of the component threads in the needle, even if it is a thick twist, otherwise when it is pulled through the threads will distort. A sling or lasso works like a metal needle threader and can be very useful when dealing with thick and multiple threads. There are several ways to create a sling. The simplest is to push the bend of a buttonhole thread through the eye of the needle, then place the stripped end of the thread into the loop and carefully pull up the loop, making sure that the metal does not fall out of the sling (see the top photograph, right). The metal thread can be either pulled right through the needle or held firmly beside the needle before pulling it through the fabric (see the bottom photograph, right).

Once the metal thread is through to the wrong side it must be fastened off, otherwise it can become entangled in the stitchery. The thread needs to be held back behind the embroidery with three or four stitches and then any spare thread trimmed back to about 12mm (½in). If possible, allow the thread to lie in the direction it was travelling in on the front; this avoids creating the effect of a hole. However, this may not be possible if the design line ends in the middle of the fabric. In this case, plunge the end and gently bend it back on itself behind the embroidery. Try to leave it slightly loose so that it 'fills' the hole made.

When working with a thick twist, it can be useful to unravel and splay the threads out flat behind the embroidery before catching them back. The ends can then be trimmed to different lengths to spread the bulk. Similarly, if many threads are being plunged in one area then it is useful to trim all of them back to differing lengths, once they have been stitched back, to stop them forming a lump.

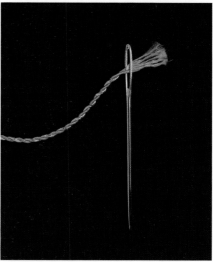

Using a sling or lasso to pass a stripped thread through a needle ready for plunging.

Holding back ends.

Crossing ends behind the embroidery.

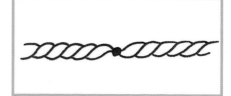

Hole effect created by ends folded back on themselves.

PEARL PURL

Pearl purl is usually abbreviated to PP and is a stiff, domed wire that is coiled to create the appearance of a row of tiny beads. Pearl purl is couched in place with another thread, usually a lightly waxed, single length of polyester or silk thread in a matching colour. It is available in several sizes from very fine to no. 4 (the largest), and as 2 per cent gold, gilt, 90 per cent silver, silver plated and copper. Coloured versions of the larger sizes are also available. Pearl purl is a very useful thread as it does not require plunging through to the wrong side.

Pearl purl is used mainly for creating boundaries or edges in a design as it is excellent for forming into an accurate shape, particularly the finer sizes. It can be carefully tweaked or pinched with tweezers for a sharp finish, however take care with the tweezers as over-zealous pinching can damage the thread. Usually, pearl purl is couched around an outline first before the enclosed area is embroidered. This stops the design expanding and becoming too chunky. Pearl purl also works well when combined with other metal threads to form patterns.

Pearl purl should be gently stretched before use, just enough to open the gaps slightly between the coils (usually the length should be increased by about one quarter). This allows the attaching thread to drop easily between the coils without distressing the metal. To stretch pearl purl, hold the cut end between your thumb and forefinger and gently stroke the metal with the thumb and forefinger of the other hand. The larger sizes of pearl purl are fairly robust but the finer sizes need to be stretched carefully to avoid over-stretching.

HOW TO APPLY PEARL PURL

The usual way to apply pearl purl is to retain the entire length and cut off any spare just before each section is completed. Occasionally, it is necessary to cut exact lengths and even pre-shape them before attaching. For added neatness, trim back the pearl purl with the scissor blades following the direction of the coils before starting to stitch.

1 Start by anchoring the attaching thread along the design line with three tiny backstitches. Position the pearl purl so that the end meets the edge of the design as none of the metal will be passed through to the back of the fabric. Couch over the pearl purl, bringing the needle up through the fabric and then going down into the same hole. Gently pull on this thread so that it disappears between the coils. Often it will make a popping sound as it passes through the pearl purl. Place a stitch in between the first two coils and continue couching at 3mm (⅛in) intervals. For difficult areas, place the couching stitches closer together.

2 Turn pearl purl by taking a stitch on the exact point where the metal needs to bend. Hold the thread taut under the frame with one hand and use the thumb or finger of the other hand to push the pearl purl back against this stitch in the desired direction. Do not pull the pearl purl as this will stretch it. Continue stitching down the pearl purl around the shape and only tweak it once it has been attached, otherwise it can ride up on top of itself.

3 When approximately 6mm (¼in) away from the end of the design line, trim off the spare pearl purl a fraction larger than required and prune off a coil at a time until the desired size is achieved (it is awkward to position the scissors without damaging the fabric if the pearl purl is already completely attached). Again, cut it in the direction of the coil for a neat finish. Continue to attach the pearl purl, making sure that there is a stitch between the last two coils.

Pearl purl.

Examples of unstretched (top) and gently stretched (bottom) pearl purl (enlarged for clarity).

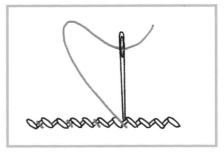

Couching down pearl purl.

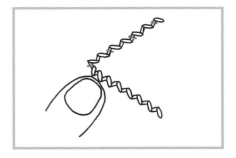

Turning pearl purl.

Note that in the two diagrams above the pearl purl is deliberately drawn over-stretched to show the stitches more clearly. Refer to the photograph second from top for the correct degree of stretching.

OVER-STRETCHING PEARL PURL

Pearl purl is normally stretched slightly to allow the stitches to drop down into the coils, becoming invisible. It can also be deliberately over-stretched to create an open effect and it is worth experimenting with the degree of stretch to produce different qualities of line. An over-stretched length of pearl purl sewn next to a traditional length can form a delicate filigree edge. Over-stretched pearl purl is usually held down with a matching metallic thread (for example, heavy metal thread) but it can also be stitched down with a contrasting coloured thread. In the latter case do keep the spaces between the stitches consistent to maintain an even appearance.

ENTWINING PEARL PURL

Once pearl purl has been deliberately over-stretched it can have another thread wound in between the coils. This could be another metallic thread, such as a T number or 3-ply twist, or coloured embroidery thread, for example perlé or stranded cotton. This is a good way of subtly introducing a colour into your embroidery. Work out the approximate length of pearl purl required before entwining it; this saves you having to unwind lots of unwanted entwined pearl purl at the end. Stitch the pearl purl down with a thread that matches the colour of the entwined thread, leaving 2.5cm (1in) tails overhanging each end that can be plunged through to the wrong side once the length is attached. When you are approximately 12mm (½in) away from the end, unwind some of the thread so that any spare pearl purl can be safely cut off without snipping the entwined thread. Wind up the remaining pearl purl and stitch it down. Now plunge the tails and tidy them off on the back.

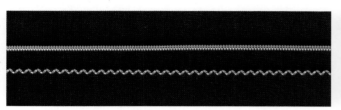

Unstretched (top) and over-stretched (bottom) pearl purl.

Entwining pearl purl.

Leave overhanging ends that can be plunged later.

COILING PEARL PURL

Pearl purl can be manipulated by coiling it around objects – needles are ideal. Large coils can be made around a no. 18 chenille needle whereas finer effects can be produced using a thin straw needle (nos. 9 or 10). Experiment with coiling the pearl purl in different ways: it can be wound either very closely or openly, or wound neatly or randomly. It can also be wound onto another thread before stitching it down. Attach the coiled pearl purl with a matching metallic thread, such as heavy metal thread, every 6mm (¼in).

TWISTING PEARL PURL TOGETHER

Lay two or more lengths of pearl purl together and twist them up. As it is a firm thread, the twist will usually stay in place. Cut the twisted threads to the desired length and attach them with invisible stitches every 6mm (¼in) using a matching metallic thread.

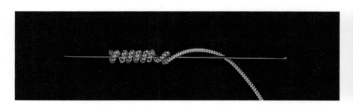

Coiling pearl purl around a needle.

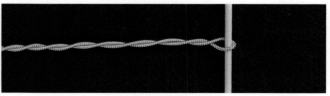

Pearl purl twisted by turning a cocktail stick.

ELIZABETHAN TWIST

Elizabethan twist is a very fine, 2-ply twist. As it is so thin, two lengths are often stitched down together when working larger shapes. It is usually held down with a single waxed coloured thread, which also forms the detailing (for example veins and edges) on the design. Keep the stitches relatively small to avoid creating too open an effect and work the stitches in a backstitch motion, making sure that they link in with the previous stitchery to form a continuous line. Always leave 5cm (2in) of Elizabethan twist overhanging the design line that can be plunged later (see page 43). This technique needs to be worked before an edging is applied.

ATTACHING ELIZABETHAN TWIST

Traditional method: couch down two strands of Elizabethan twist together, laying them alongside each other for better coverage. Starting at either the top or the bottom of a leaf, for example, leave a 5cm (2in) tail and take the first stitch over the twist at one edge of the leaf, and the second stitch at the other edge. Bend the twist and take another stitch over it to begin the next row. Bring the needle out a little away from the previous stitch, take it over the twist and go down into the same hole as the previous stitch. Work across the leaf, taking stitches at each side. Continue like this, working back and forth across the shape, adding in vein lines as they are needed. If necessary, work a few backstitches just through the fabric to complete the outline.

Diagonal method: this method is similar to the traditional method, but the stitches are worked diagonally down each side from the edge to the vein. Pay particular attention to the angle of the stitches and complete the edge with a few backstitches through the fabric only.

Diagonal over card: similar to the diagonal method, here two pieces of card are lightly glued to the fabric first, leaving a gap down the middle as a centre vein. Attach the Elizabethan twist with a single stitch at each side using a thread that matches the metal. This gives a padded satin stitch effect.

Flowing from the delicate wild rose flower worked in silk shading, the leaves embroidered in diagonal Elizabethan twist enhance the soft feel of the design giving an overall balance to the piece. See also pages 78–79.

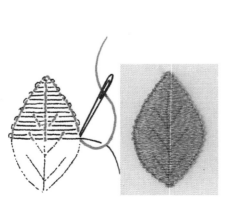

Traditional method.

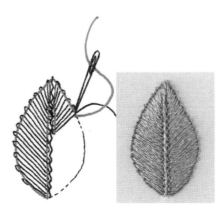

Diagonal method.

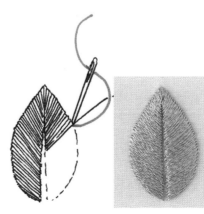

Diagonal over card.

KID

Kid can provide an excellent focal point in a design, especially for church work where boldness is required, but it can dominate. You therefore need to think carefully about how much to apply and where to apply it. If the kid is to be placed over padding, it is worth cutting out the shape slightly larger than required and trimming it back if it is too large. Use a metallic sewing thread (heavy metal thread) to attach the kid as this will blend into the surface. Much of the attaching stitchery can be hidden with a goldwork edging such as pearl purl or milliary.

TRANSFERRING A DESIGN ONTO KID

Trace off the shape and carefully cut out the tracing. Lay the tracing on the right side of the kid and place some low-tack tape across it to hold it in place. Carefully cut out the shape from the right side, taking the scissors right up to the edge of the tracing. This produces a clean edge to the leather and ensures that the shape is the right way round – essential if you are cutting out initials!

ATTACHING KID

A large piece of kid can be held in place temporarily before it is attached using three or four stitches that go right across the shape. Use a contrasting thread to make it easier to determine which stitches to remove later on. Kid is sewn down in the same way as felt padding (see page 20). Use small stitches, coming up through the fabric and going down into the kid at a 45-degree angle. This avoids damaging the kid too much as the needle is passed through it and therefore gives the neatest finish. Begin by placing one stitch in each quarter, working north, south, east and west, then add the stitches in between. Large pieces of kid may require more than four preliminary stitches.

Transferring the design.

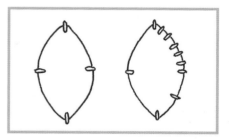

Attaching kid using four holding stitches then placing the remaining stitches in between.

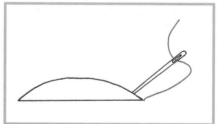

Place the stitches at a 45-degree angle.

The wings of the bat have been applied with soft black leather, chosen as it adds a natural texture and sheen to the surface of the wings. The edges and veins are highlighted with couched silver T371 stitched down with silver heavy metal thread no. 30, to add further depth and definition to the wings (see also pages 146–147).

BROAD, 11'S AND WHIPPED PLATE

Broad plate is a wide strip of flattened metal with a ribbon-like appearance. 11's plate is a narrower version. Two per cent gold broad plate is the easiest to work with as gilt, silver and copper versions are quite soft and can buckle. Whipped plate is a broad plate that has been wrapped with a fine metal wire. This makes the strip firmer, so either quality is easy to work with.

Broad plate, 11's and whipped plate can be attached in straight lines, or laid in a grid pattern or zigzag formation, either closed or open. Interesting light effects can be created by twisting the plate by hand before sewing it down. Alternatively, try slotting the plate into the open eye of a needle and winding it around the needle to form scrolls. You can also do this using a quilling tool.

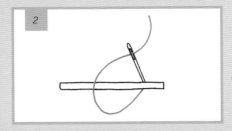

ATTACHING BROAD, 11'S AND WHIPPED PLATE

Use a single waxed polyester thread in a toning colour to attach the hooks, but any thread can be worked with for the couching stitches depending on whether the stitches are to be decorative or merely functional. Once attached, the plates can be embellished with cut pieces of purl.

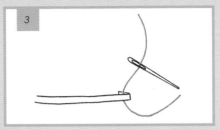

1 Each end of the plate needs to be stitched down before you start couching. Begin by making a small hook or barb about 3mm (⅛in) long at the end of the plate. Use a pair of flat-ended tweezers to gently fold the plate back on itself. Take care, as none of the turned-under plate should show.

2 Lay the plate across the fabric, letting it overhang the design line. Use the plate as a guide for the width of the anchoring stitch. Bring the needle up below the plate and take it down above it, but do not pull up the stitch.

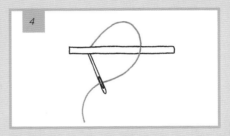

3 Carefully remove the plate and place the hook into the looped stitch. Gently pull up the attaching thread while retaining tension on the plate to bring the hook to the fabric. Take a tiny stab stitch where it will not be seen to hold the plate taut.

4 Gently lay the plate against the fabric again and bring the needle up on the design line at the other end of the plate. Make a stitch the width of the plate but again leave it as a loop. Cut the plate off slightly beyond the design line.

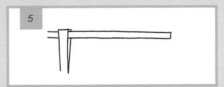

5 Bend under the excess with the tweezers and place the hook into the loop.

6 Maintain the tension by inserting a mellore, stiletto or a large needle while pulling on the loop. Again use a small holding stitch to secure this stitch.

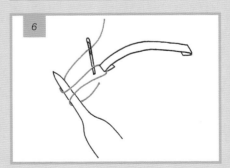

7 Couch over the plate with the chosen thread and stitch. Stitch some pieces of cut purl across the plate if desired. Make sure that the attaching stitch is the same length as the cut purl otherwise it will arc or the attaching thread will show.

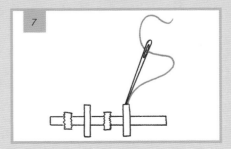

ZIGZAGS

A zigzag effect can be worked with the plate either spaced apart or close together, and either flat against the fabric or stitched over padding. Start in the usual way with a hook (see opposite) and when a bend is required take a stitch over the plate at that point. Hold the stitching thread firmly from underneath the frame and bend back the plate against the stitch. Make a tiny stab stitch where it will be hidden to secure it. Smooth the plate by either rubbing your thumb over it or gently stroking it with the paddle-end of a mellore and take the next stitch over the plate, bending the plate in the opposite direction to create the zigzag. Continue in this way until the last bend and secure the end with a hook.

If working a closed zigzag, slightly overlap each section of the zigzag with the previous one and stitch it down with a backstitch motion.

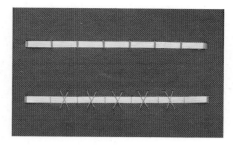

Broad plate held down with coloured stranded cotton and heavy metal thread.

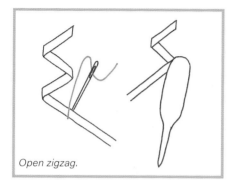

Open zigzag.

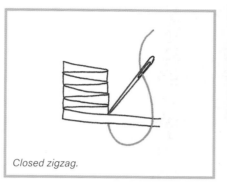

Closed zigzag.

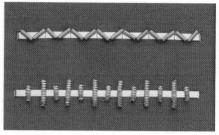

Broad plate decorated with pieces of bright check purl and rough purl.

Chevron patterns can be achieved by laying two zigzag formations together. This can be decorated with small lengths of purl. A more experimental approach is to lay the plate in haphazard, random directions (see right).

Random zigzag 11's plate.

The bottom section of the butterfly body is worked using zigzag plate, which adds both depth and lustre to the finished piece of work whilst looking accurate to nature as well (see also pages 142–143).

Goldwork Wild Rose

Hazel designed this wild rose to highlight the variety of effects that can be achieved with different techniques and threads. This one has been worked in all gold, but it could easily be worked in corresponding coloured metal threads. It was worked by one of Hazel's students, Clare Phelan.

FABRIC

- Cream silk dupion: 25 x 35cm (10 x 14in)
- Calico: 25 x 35cm (10 x 14in)

THREADS (ALL GOLD)

- Gold heavy metal no. 30
- Gold Ophir
- No. 6 smooth passing: 1m (39in)
- Check thread no. 7: 1.5m (59in)
- 3-ply twist: 1m (39in)
- Bright check purl no. 6: 1m (39in)
- Smooth purl no. 6: 50cm (20in)

TECHNIQUES

- Shaded chippings (see page 32)
- Purl loops (see page 35)
- Graded cutwork (see page 33)
- Couched threads (see pages 36–38)
- Twists (see page 39)
- Satin stitch (see page 75)

TEMPLATE

See page 172

ORDER OF WORK

Use gold heavy metal thread no. 30 for sewing thread throughout.

1 Transfer the design onto the fabric using your desired method. Mark the stems as single lines only. (The dotted line is only to indicate the placement of the check no. 7 thread – do not mark this on the fabric). Frame up the fabric with the calico backing.

2 Couch the 3-ply twist along the stems, starting with the central stem – leave 2.5cm (1in) tails at the beginning and end of each section (do not use one continuous piece for all the stems as it will be too lumpy behind your work). Couch check thread no. 7 along the areas marked by the dotted lines on the design, as close to the twist as possible, again leaving 2.5cm (1in) tails at the beginning and end. When all the stems are completed, plunge the tails down through the fabric and oversew behind the embroidery.

3 Outline the main flower with smooth passing no. 6, starting with the petals in the foreground and working back (see the stitch-order diagram, right). Cut a 50cm (20in) length of passing. Start at the centre of the flower leaving a 2.5cm (1in) tail at the beginning (to plunge later). When the central circle is completed, take the passing thread through the fabric and bring it up at the beginning of petal no. 2, being careful to angle your needle to allow the thread to fit smoothly to the centre line. Couch around the petal, then take the thread down at the end of the petal and bring it up at the start of the next. Repeat this until the flower is completely outlined, and leaving a 2.5cm (1in) tail at the end. Take the start and end tails of the passing through the fabric and oversew them behind the embroidery.

4 Couch the passing around the two buds in the same way.

5 Outline each leaf in check thread no. 7, starting and ending with a 2.5cm (1in) tail at the stem every time. Plunge all ends when completed and oversew behind the embroidery.

6 Fill each petal with very tiny chippings using both purls. Place the bright check purl near the centre and shaded areas and the smooth purl towards the edge of the flower in the lighter areas.

7 Embroider the bud sepals with satin stitch in gold Ophir. Fill the buds with very tiny chippings in smooth purl.

8 Fill the centre of the flower with loopy chippings about 5mm (¼in) long in both bright check and smooth purls, randomly placed.

9 Work the inside of the leaves in diagonal cutwork in bright check purl.

Goldwork Violet

This piece was designed and worked by Hazel in the spring of 2018. It shows
how beautiful, natural and versatile metal thread embroidery can be.

FABRIC

- Ivory silk: 25 x 35cm (10 x 14in)
- Calico: 25 x 35cm (10 x 14in)

THREADS

- Gold 8 x 2 check thread:
  1m (39in)
- Gilt smooth passing no. 6:
  3m (119in)
- Gold wire check purl no. 8:
  5cm (2in)
- Silver rough purl no. 8: 1m (39in)
- Lavender rough purl no. 8:
  1m (39in)
- Lilac rough purl no. 8: 1m (39in)
- Light green rough purl no. 8:
  1m (39in)
- Dark green rough purl no. 8:
  1m (39in)
- Gold heavy metal no. 30
- Invisible thread
- Gold Ophir

TECHNIQUES

- Couched threads (see pages
  36–38)
- Shaded chippings (see page 32)
- Fuzzy effect (see page 32)

TEMPLATE

See page 172

ORDER OF WORK

1 Transfer the design onto the background fabric using your chosen method. Mark the stems as single lines only. Frame up with the calico backing.

2 Outline the large open leaf with 8 x 2 check thread, couching it down with gold heavy metal no. 30. Begin at the indent at the back of the leaf, leaving 2.5cm (1in) for plunging at the start and end.

3 Outline the two folded leaves with 8 x 2 check thread, starting at the stalk. Join and finish at the turnover, again leaving 2.5cm (1in) tails for plunging.

4 Edge the flower petals and the bud with smooth passing no. 6, couching with gold heavy metal no. 30. Start with the petals in the foreground and finish with the petals at the back, and leave 2.5cm (1in) tails for plunging.

5 Create the stems from smooth passing no. 6: apply a single length for the flower stalks and two separate lengths for the leaf stalks. Plunge and sew back all the tails.

6 Embroider all the petals with tiny chippings of coloured purl. Start with the silver on the edges and then work a shadow area in lavender and lilac, blending the colours to add depth.

7 Fill the sepals with tiny chips of light and dark green purl.

8 Work the centre of the flower in gold wire check chips.

9 Fill the leaf spaces with fuzzy effect in light and dark green purl shading, and where appropriate tie down with invisible thread.

10 Finish by adding vein lines in gold Ophir thread to the large leaf, couched down with gold heavy metal no. 30.

THREE-DIMENSIONAL GOLDWORK

If you would like to complement a design with three-dimensional elements there are a number of things to consider.

1 It is easier to use bold shapes with smoother edges, otherwise finishing the three-dimensional element can be difficult.

2 You need to think carefully about your overall design and how the elements will all fit together.

3 Some parts of the design need to be worked independently on separate pieces of fabric and then applied. It is important to break down the design, remembering the general rules of goldwork (see page 25).

4 Applying the separate three-dimensional elements is always the last stage of work.

5 Planning and breaking your design into sections is very important when adding lots of padding and three-dimensional elements to ensure your design flows naturally. This is not a technique for a beginner. I would advise you master goldwork techniques before you attempt to add three-dimensional elements.

Goldwork 3D Christmas Rose

Designed by Hazel; worked by Jan.

FABRIC

- Dark green silk dupion: 30 x 30cm (12 x 12in)
- Calico, two pieces: 30 x 30cm (12 x 12in)
- Yellow felt: 10 x 10cm (4 x 4in)
- Gold kid: 5 x 5cm (2 x 2in)

THREADS

- Gold heavy metal no. 30
- Gold Ophir
- Gold pearl purl: 50cm (20in)
- Gold 3-ply twist: 75cm (29½in)
- Gold passing no. 4: 225cm (88½in)
- Gilt fine rococco: 75cm (29½in)
- Smooth gilt purl no. 8: 50cm (20in)

TECHNIQUES

- Stacked fly stitch (see page 75)
- Couched threads (see pages 36–38)
- Twists (see page 39)
- Purl chippings (see page 31)
- Kid (see page 47)
- Felt padding (see page 20)

TEMPLATES

See page 173

ORDER OF WORK

1 Transfer just the leaves and two petals onto the silk dupion fabric using your chosen method. These are the only bits worked directly on the fabric. Frame up with one of the calico backing pieces.

2 For the two-dimensional petals, pad with two layers of felt.

3 The leaves are embroidered directly onto the fabric in stacked fly stitch in gold Ophir.

4 For the two-dimensional petals, work directly over the felt padding. Outline the petals with pearl purl starting and ending at the centre, couched down with gold heavy metal no. 30.

5 Continue using gold heavy metal no. 30 as the sewing thread and add a row of 3-ply twist couched inside the pearl purl, followed by three rows of smooth passing no. 4, then a row of gilt fine rococco. Then add a further three rows of smooth passing no. 4. Remember to leave 2.5cm (1in) tails at the start and finish of each to plunge and fasten behind the embroidery. Infill any space left with tiny chips of smooth gilt no. 8 purl. Plunge the ends and fasten back behind each petal.

6 For the three front petals, transfer each petal design onto the remaining piece of calico, leaving a 2.5cm (1in) gap between the petals to allow for cutting out. Frame up.

7 Embroider each of the three front petals in the same way as the two back petals. Once the embroidery is complete, cut the excess calico away leaving a 5mm (¼in) seam allowance around each petal. Turn this seam allowance under and sew it back behind each petal.

8 Position the petals on the background fabric. Plunge the tails from the couched threads of the petals and fasten off behind the work; these help to anchor the petals in position. Then stitch the petals in place using small oversew stitches along the centre edge; using gold heavy metal thread allows the stitches to disappear and be hidden.

9 For the flower centre, cut out a circle from the kid with a diameter of about 12mm (½in) (this may need trimming to size) and stitch into place. Outline with 3-ply twist, taking great care when plunging the tails to make the join as seamless as possible.

SILK SHADING

Silk shading has been seen throughout history, from the rich silk embroideries of the Far East to the ornate ecclesiastical vestments of Europe, embodying wealth and opulence. Today it is often referred to as 'painting with a needle', as the embroiderer's goal is to create an image as close to reality as possible. When worked correctly, the embroidery will look like a painting.

Silk shading was, as the name implies, originally worked in fine, loosely spun thread such as silk. This added to its opulence and expense. In more recent times, however, with the invention of other threads such as stranded cottons, which are an ideal substitute for silk, it can be a relatively cheap form of embroidery. Stranded cottons are readily available and modern dyes provide a wealth of colours with many shades in each range. This enables the embroiderer to blend colour seamlessly, adding shape, depth and definition to their work without the need for padding. As silk is no longer the only choice of thread, in many cases silk shading is often referred to as long-and-short stitch embroidery.

RULES FOR SILK SHADING

1 Generally, silk shading is worked from the background moving forwards. This enables the foreground shapes to have smooth, accurate outlines. If you work from front to back, there is a danger that the new stitches will affect the line and damage the smooth lay of the thread.

2 Use short lengths of thread up to 45cm (18in). This prevents wear on the thread, which may cause it to dull or split, ruining the silkiness. Try not to handle the thread too much as this can cause it to lose its lustre.

3 Finish the thread before it becomes damaged. If you try and eke out every last bit of thread, although tempting, this can cause it to become ragged and therefore appear matt instead of shiny.

4 Always keep all spare working threads on the top surface of the fabric, as any threads at the back of the work can get caught up with subsequent stitching and become tangled.

5 Start and finish a thread wherever possible with two or three stab stitches within an area that will later be covered with embroidery. When this is not possible, fasten a thread by overcasting on the back of the work either through only the calico or through any nearby stitchery.

6 If your working thread begins to tangle, allow the needle to fall on the wrong side of the work and it will spiral and untangle itself.

7 Make sure you have a good number of shades in each colour to allow for smooth, soft transitions unless you require obvious colour effects.

8 Always cover your work and spare threads when you have a break from your embroidery as this will keep them clean. The natural light can also discolour threads and therefore change the appearance you are trying to create.

9 Remember when your work is complete that direct sunlight and damp are not good for it, so place it carefully with this in mind.

10 Silk shading does not require padding, but to enhance your work and to create a more three-dimensional effect, use split stitch around the outer edge of your shape. This helps to form and edge the stitches, adding the illusion of depth and providing a smooth edge.

ORDER OF WORK

It is very important to start with the background sections of the design and gradually work towards the foreground or uppermost sections.

Always try to think of the subject of your image and how it appears in nature. Imagine all the separate elements and how they join together. If possible, go and study the object in nature so that you can observe how the light affects it and how its tones blend together.

Each section of a design should have a number when planning and this gives you the order of work. Methodically work through each of the numbers in numerical order. This will allow a natural depth to develop as each section will rest against an existing area of embroidery. As seen in the design below, there may be more than one of a particular number – this simply means that it does not matter in which order that particular number is worked, but that all those same numbers must be worked before moving onto the next number.

Looking at the design below, the flower is resting upon three leaves, so the leaves would be the first section to embroider and so are labelled no. 1.

An easy way to work out the correct order for the petals is to look at each of them individually. The most complete petal will be in the foreground and therefore worked last. The least complete petal will be in the background and worked first.

The petals in this design are in two roundels, with three petals laying over another three, with them alternating to form a balanced pattern. The bottom roundel of partial petals would be worked next after the leaves and are labelled no. 2. The roundel of top three petals is worked last; these petals are labelled no. 3. (The threads used for the flower are DMC stranded cotton 469, 470, 471, 472, 741, 742, 743, 744, and 976.) The flower centre is worked last. For this design, the centre was finished with French knots.

58

Silk shading threads

Threads used for silk shading need to be glossy and loosely twisted so that
each stitch merges with the next to create a smooth, blended finish.
There are many threads available such as silk, floss and cotton.

Natural silks are available in a beautiful range of colours and are incredibly soft. They can be difficult to work with and it is hard to achieve a truly smooth glossy blend and overall finish. Floss silks can be a challenge to work with, as they can catch and shed, losing their sheen.

Stranded cottons have a huge palette of over 500 colours and they are one of my personal favourites for this type of embroidery. They come as one thread made up of six strands and they have been used throughout this book. Stranded cottons merge together effortlessly, forming a smooth, shiny effect, and they are colourfast so there is no danger of running. They are also easy to work with, as they are relatively robust and do not easily catch. Stranded cottons can be found in most haberdasheries and craft shops and are relatively inexpensive.

All the silk shaded samples in the book are worked in DMC stranded cotton, but other brands are available. A crewel or embroidery needle is used for silk shading as these needles have long eyes to accommodate the soft thread.

Silk shading techniques

SPLIT STITCH

Why use a split stitch? Split stitch is a very useful stitch that is used in conjunction with long-and-short stitch in silk shading. It is used to create a smooth boundary or edge to shapes, and it is used to form a lift between sections or shapes. It is a foundation stitch and is always worked in the same colour as the long-and-short stitch that will cover it, or in the colour that is most dominant. It is always worked with the same thickness of thread used throughout the piece: if you used one strand of stranded cotton for the long-and-short stitch, you would also use one strand of stranded cotton for the split stitch. The long-and-short stitch always entirely covers the split stitch. There are two different ways to create this stitch (see below). Both are valid, you just need to choose which works best for you.

METHOD 1

Fasten on the thread and make a stitch that is approximately 3mm (⅛in) long (the length can vary depending upon the scale of the design). Bring the needle back up through the middle of the stitch by piercing it from underneath (**A**). Pull the thread up and then make a new stitch by going down into the fabric about 2mm (⅟₁₆in) on from the last stitch (**B**). Bring the needle back up through the centre of the newly made stitch. Proceed in this way, piercing the new stitching from beneath. I use this method as I find it gives me more directional control.

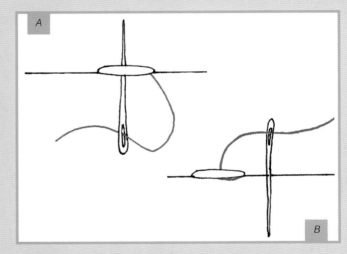

METHOD 2

This second method is more popular, as it is easier to pierce the stitch more accurately by going down into it. Fasten on the thread and make a stitch that is approximately 3mm (⅛in) long. Bring the needle back up through the fabric approximately 2mm (⅟₁₆in) beyond the end of the first stitch. Then take the needle down into the middle of the stitch, piercing through the thread. Continue in this manner by always splitting the stitches from above. This is an easier version to control.

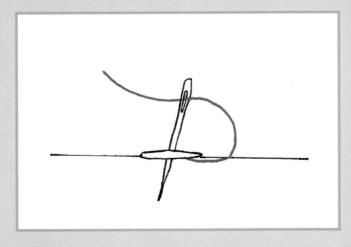

SILK SHADING

Coloured thread shading can be achieved in different ways. The tulip design below shows the very popular natural shading on the leaves, perpendicular tapestry shading on the tulip flower and satin stitch block shading on the stem. It was worked in DMC stranded cotton colours: 321, 469, 470, 471, 472, 666, 814, 815 and 816. This project was designed by Hazel and worked by Jan.

Tapestry shading: the tulip flower
This is where the stitches run vertically throughout the design. It is most often used for figures in ecclesiastical and heraldic embroidery. It can produce some very realistic designs as the stitches vary in length to create a painterly effect.

Block shading: the stem
This displays definite seams and ridges where the work has been overlaid. It is usually worked in satin stitch (see page 75) with the needle going down in the previous stitch. The idea is to produce bold blocks of colour in a stylized way, creating voids and bands of colour. It is a very striking effect.

Natural or soft shading: the leaves
This is the most popular method used and is where the stitches follow the flow of the separate elements of the design. It is usually found in natural forms, creating a realistic piece of embroidery. The stitches should be closely packed together and follow the direction of the design to produce a softly blended piece of embroidery.

BLOCK SHADING

Block shading is not long-and-short stitch or silk shading in its truest sense. However, it is a technique that fits well in this section. This technique is worked in sections and provides a striking effect. To practise this, use DMC 554 (light), DMC 553 (medium) and DMC 550 (dark), with one strand throughout.

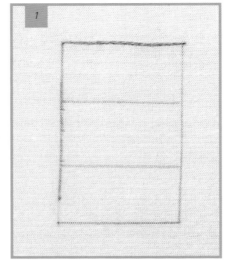

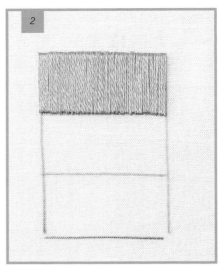

1 Draw a rectangle measuring 1 x 3cm (½ x 1¼in). Divide it vertically into thirds. Split stitch across the top edge using one strand of DMC 554 (this split-stitching process can be repeated at each colour change if a more defined line of change is required).

2 Satin stitch the top third in DMC 554 (see page 75 for guidance on satin stitching). Come up in the fabric and down over the split stitch, keeping the stitches parallel to the sides of the rectangle. Work across the shape from right to left. It is important that you always work in the same direction to give the smoothest overall finish.

3 For the middle third, change to DMC 553. Work in exactly the same way as for the top third.

4 Change to DMC 550 for the final third and work in the same way as for the middle third.

Tip

If you want to work with two strands, work in exactly the same way but with two strands in the needle at the same time.

TAPESTRY SHADING

All the stitches worked run vertically within the design. This can be challenging in some designs as it is hard to keep the stitch formation straight.

For this exercise, draw a small square approximately 2.5cm (1in) in size. Choose three colours in DMC stranded cotton: one light, one medium and one dark.

With long-and-short stitch, the idea is to create a smooth effect that seamlessly blends together. However, for this practice sample, the colour changes will show up in the rows as there are only three different shades and they are very different. In order to achieve a seamless blend, the colour changes should be very slight. For this example, however, having very different shades will help to see the changes. Here the samples are worked in DMC 554 (light), DMC 553 (medium) and DMC 550 (dark).

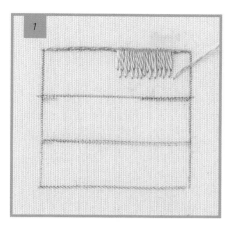

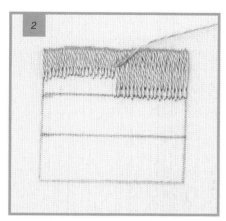

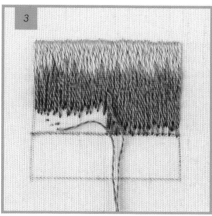

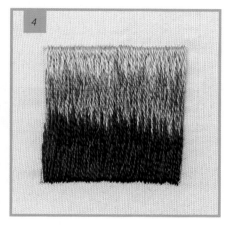

Tip

To help with blending you can work in two strands of DMC stranded cotton. This is completed in the same way, but to aid blending use:

Rows 1 and 2: two strands of DMC 554.

Row 3: one strand of DMC 554 and one strand of DMC 553.

Row 4: two strands of DMC 553.

Row 5: one strand of DMC 553 and one strand of DMC 550.

Row 6: two strands of DMC 550 to complete the square.

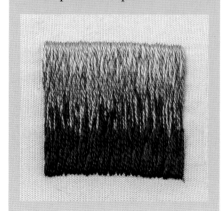

1 Divide the square into thirds with a 2H pencil. Using one strand of DMC 554, work split stitch along the top edge to form a smooth line. Bring the needle up in the centre of the square, halfway down the first third, and take it back down over the split stitch, angling the needle under the split stitch to form a smooth edge. There is greater control and accuracy in taking the needle down into the fabric on the edge of the design – it gives a sharper finish. Work the stitches with one long then one short stitch, alternating from the centre out. The stitches should be worked very closely together so no background fabric can be seen. When one side is complete, work the other side from the centre out.

2 Starting in the centre of the first row, bring the needle up one third of the way into the previous stitches and bring it down into the fabric over the drawn line. Alternating between long and short stitches, work across the square to the edge, keeping the stitches very close together. Then return to the centre and work to the other side to complete the row. Bringing the needle up through the first stitches gives a smoother end result. If you require a more defined finish for elements such as fur, come up in the fabric and go down into the previous row (just make sure you keep the same technique throughout the piece of work – if you combine both methods you will be able to see the slight variation on your finished piece).

3 Change the thread to DMC 553. Work in the same way as row two, coming up in the stitch and down in the fabric. Work two rows in this colour to finish the second third.

4 Change colour again to DMC 550 and work in the same way to complete the final third. Secure the thread by running it through the back of the work.

NATURAL SHADING

As the name suggests, natural shading follows the shape that is being worked. It can be a good idea to draw out the stitch direction and the shading before you start to work to help keep the form.

Here, all the top outer edges are outlined with split stitch to add definition and depth to the design. This should be worked in the same thread colour and with the same thickness as the thread used for the long-and-short stitch. To practise, draw a shape taken from your actual piece of embroidery. In this case, the Silk Shaded 3D Christmas Rose petal from page 173.

I am only using three shades: a light, medium and dark to show clearly how to blend. To aid the smooth blending of tones when working properly, shades in between these should be used for a seamless effect. I used one strand throughout of DMC 554, DMC 553 and DMC 550.

1 Divide the shape into three sections with a 2H pencil. Split stitch around the top outer edge using one strand of DMC 554. Do not split stitch along the base of the petal.

2 For the first row, begin with one strand of DMC 554. Start in the middle of the row by bringing the needle up in the main body of the petal and taking it down over the split stitch, angling the needle under the split stitch to form a smooth, accurate edge. Work to one side of the petal with alternating long then short stitches, placing them close together so that you cannot see any background fabric. Try to make the stitches as irregular in length as possible, as this will produce the best effect.

3 Return to the centre and complete the first row in the same way, working out to the other side. Row 2 is worked in the same way using DMC 554, but by bringing the needle up at least a third of the way up the previous stitch, physically splitting the thread. The length of the stitches may vary in order to give the smooth effect. Start in the middle of the shape each time to help with the stitch direction.

4 Rows 3 and 4 should be worked in the same way as row 2, using DMC 553. Sometimes the needle may need to be taken quite high into the previous row of stitches to create a more staggered and natural effect, giving a gradual change of colour.

5 Complete the petal (row 5) in the same way as previous rows using DMC 550.

Tip

If you decide to work in two strands of DMC then work as left but in this colour sequence:

Row 1: two strands of DMC 554.

Row 2: one strand of DMC 554 and one strand of DMC 553.

Row 3: two strands of DMC 553.

Row 4: one strand of DMC 553 and one strand of DMC 550.

Row 5: two strands of DMC 550.

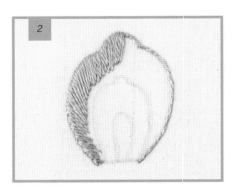

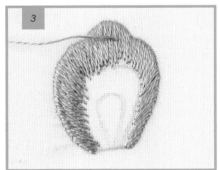

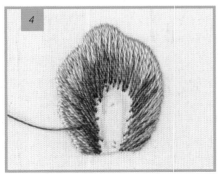

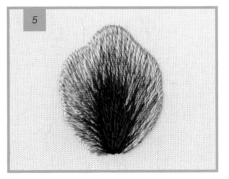

NATURAL SHADING WITH DEFINITION

Occasionally it is appropriate to have a slightly harder finish to the normal seamless natural effect of long-and-short stitch. One example of this is animal fur. In this case, the stitches need to look like independent strands of hair and thus more defined. In order to achieve this the long-and-short stitch is worked in the same direction and with the same shading effect as natural long-and-short stitch. However, rather than coming up through the previous row of stitches and down in the fabric the process is reversed: you bring up the needle in the fabric and take it down through the previous row of stitches. Here, I used DMC 554, DMC 553 and DMC 550.

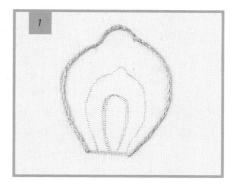

1 Use the same petal shape as on page 64. Divide the petal into thirds with a 2H pencil. Using one strand of DMC 554, work split stitch around the outer top edge. Do not split stitch the petal base.

2 For the first row, begin with one strand of DMC 554. Start in the middle of the row by bringing the needle up in the main body of the petal and taking it down over the split stitch, forming a smooth, accurate edge. Work to one side of the petal with alternating long then short stitches, placing them close together so that you cannot see any background fabric. Try to make the stitches as irregular in length as possible, as this will produce the best effect. Remember that for each of the subsequent rows you will be bringing up the needle in the fabric and then taking it down through the previous row of stitches, covering about a third of the previous stitch.

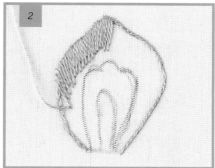

3 Return to the centre and complete the first row in the same way, working out to the other side. Row 2 is worked in the same way using DMC 554, by bringing the needle up in the fabric in the middle of the petal and taking it down at least a third of the way up the previous stitch. The length of the stitches may vary in order to give a smooth effect.

4 Rows 3 and 4 should be worked in the same way as rows 1 and 2, using DMC 553. Sometimes the needle may need to be taken quite high into the previous row of stitches to create a more staggered and natural effect, giving a gradual change of colour.

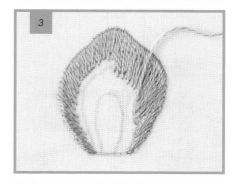

5 Complete the petal (row 5) in the same way as previous rows using DMC 550.

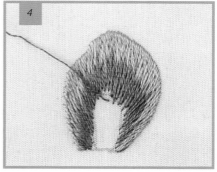

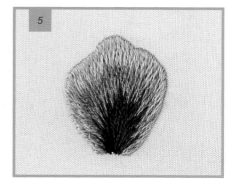

Tip

If you decide to work in two strands of DMC, work as above but in this colour sequence:

Row 1: two strands of DMC 554.

Row 2: one strand of DMC 554 and one strand of DMC 553.

Row 3: two strands of DMC 553.

Row 4: one strand of DMC 553 and one strand of DMC 550.

Row 5: two strands of DMC 550.

Silk Shaded Wild Rose

This is the same design as on pages 50–51, worked in goldwork, and on pages 78–79 in a combination of goldwork and silk shading. Hazel designed this rose to show not only its beauty but also its versatility when stitched in different mediums. The silk-shaded rose shows how natural and effective this form of embroidery can be. Worked by Elaine Brum.

FABRIC

- Cream silk dupion: 25 x 35cm (10 x 14in)
- Calico: 25 x 35cm (10 x 14in)

THREADS

DMC stranded cotton
- Flower: 3687, 3688, 3689, 819
- Centre: 726, 783
- Leaves and stems: 986, 987, 988, 989

TECHNIQUES

- Long-and-short stitch natural shading (see page 64)
- Split stitch (see page 60)
- French knots (see page 76)
- Stem stitch (see page 74)
- Satin stitch (see page 75)

TEMPLATE

See page 172

ORDER OF WORK

Use one strand of thread throughout unless otherwise stated.

1 Transfer the design onto the background fabric using your chosen method and mark the stems. Frame up the fabric with the calico backing.

2 Work the stems in two strands of 987 using a small stem stitch.

3 The no. 2 and 3 leaves are worked in a combination of 986, 987, 988 and 989. Firstly, split stitch around the outer edge of the no. 2 leaves with 987 (do not split stitch any edges that go under another part of the design). Secondly, long-and-short stitch from the point of the leaves to their bases using a combination of the greens to provide shading (refer to the direction diagram, below right). Repeat for the no. 3 leaves.

4 The buds are next (no. 4 on the diagram) and are worked in a combination of 3688 and 3687. Split stitch around the outer edge in 3688. Fill the buds with long-and-short stitch, working from the point downwards in the two colours (refer to the direction diagram, below right). For the bud sepals, split stitch all around in 987 and fill with satin stitch.

5 The petals (nos. 5, 6, 7 and 8 on the diagram) are worked in a combination of 3687, 3688, 3689 and 819. Firstly, split stitch around the outer edge of petal 5 (do not stitch areas that will be under other petals) in 819. Complete the petal with shaded long-and-short stitch, starting at the top edge of the petal and working to the centre using the four pinks (refer to the direction diagram, below right). Repeat for petals 6, 7 and 8.

6 Fill the centre of the rose with French knots worked in a random pattern using 726 and 783. You can use one or two strands here depending on personal preference; in this piece only one strand is used.

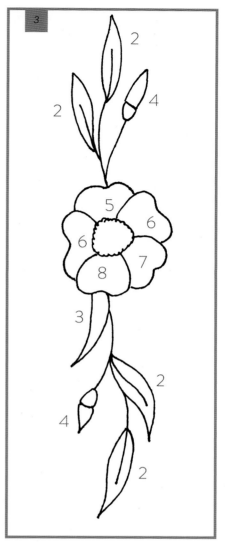

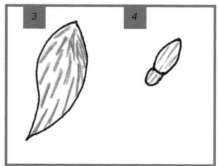

Silk Shaded Violet

Hazel liked to adapt designs so that they could be versatile. This is based
on her violet design (seen in full in the goldwork section on pages 52–53),
which has been simplified and lends itself perfectly to a beautiful silk-
shading piece. This piece was designed by Hazel and worked by Jan.

FABRIC

- Ivory silk: 25 x 25cm (10 x 10in)
- Calico: 25 x 25cm (10 x 10in)

THREADS

DMC stranded cotton

- Flower: 550, 208, 209, 210, 211, 445
- Leaves and stems: 986, 987, 988, 989

TECHNIQUES

- Split stitch (see page 60)
- Stem stitch (see page 74)
- Long-and-short stitch natural shading (see page 64)
- French knots (see page 76)

TEMPLATE

See page 172

ORDER OF WORK

1 Transfer the design onto the fabric using your chosen method. Frame up the fabric with the calico backing.

2 Working from the background forwards, begin with the stems. Use two strands of 989 and stem stitch the three stems: stem stitch one row for the flower stem and two rows, worked next to each other, for the leaf stems.

3 Next embroider the turnover leaf. Split stitch around the outside under section using one strand of 988. Complete the under section with long-and-short stitch natural shading using single strands of 988, 987 and 986 (see **3a** for the stitch direction). Split stitch right around the turnover using one strand of 989. Complete with long-and-short stitch worked in natural shading using single strands of 989, 988 and 987 (see **3b** for the stitch direction).

4 Split stitch around the large front leaf using one strand of 989. Complete the leaf in long-and-short stitch natural shading, working from the point using single strands of 989, 988, 987 and 986. See the diagram for direction (right).

5 Work each petal in the same way, referring to the diagram for the stitch order (see below right). Split stitch the outside edge of the petal using one strand of 211. Using single strands of 211, 210, 209, 208 and 550, use long-and-short stitch natural shading to infill each petal.

6 Using one strand of 445, fill in the centre of the violet with French knots. Add one or two French knots in 550 to highlight the centre.

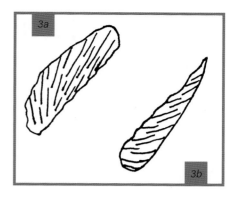

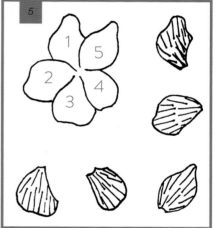

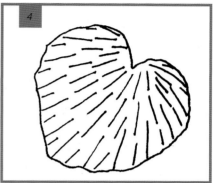

ADDING A THREE-DIMENSIONAL ELEMENT

Here is some general advice for adding three-dimensional elements, such as flower petals.

1 Couch a fine beading wire (such as 34 gauge) a little way inside the design line (about 2mm or 1/16in), leaving 2.5cm (1in) tails at the start and finish at the petal base; these will be used to attach the three-dimensional element to the background embroidery.

2 Work a row of very close buttonhole stitch (see page 74) around the edge, working over the wire edge. Make the stitches different lengths, as this helps the edge of the element stay together. When joining a new thread, be careful where you start and finish – it needs to be inside the wire and brought up through the previous top loop for a seamless join.

3 When the buttonhole edge is complete, you can work long-and-short stitch in the normal way, with the outer row going over the wire and into the loops of the buttonhole. Be careful not to pass the loops of the buttonhole (these form the outer edge of the element).

4 When your stitching is complete, carefully cut out your shape. I will cut the general shape out first with a bit of a fabric border, and then cut much closer from the right side, angling the scissors under the buttonhole loops at a 45-degree angle. Be very careful not to cut the stitches. Adding a fine metal thread such as pearl purl around the exposed edges helps to hide the cut fabric edge.

5 The pieces are then attached to the base fabric. Position the piece and plunge the wire through the fabric to hold it in place. Oversew the wire behind the fabric, making sure this is in an area covered by embroidery as you do not want to see any stitches or bulges on the front of the work. If necessary, to strengthen the area attached to the base fabric, oversew a few stitches along the join to add strength.

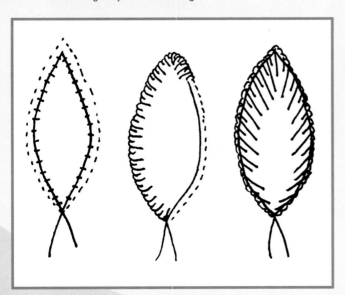

Silk Shaded 3D Christmas Rose

Designed and worked by Hazel.

FABRIC

- Fine calico: 30 x 30cm (12 x 12in)
- White fabric: 5 x 5cm (2 x 2in)
- Background fabric of your choice: 30 x 30cm (12 x 12in)
- White felt: 5 x 5cm (2 x 2in)

THREADS

- Gold wire check purl no. 8: 10cm (4in)
- Fine wire: 105cm (41½in)

DMC stranded cotton
- Leaves: 3364, 3363
- Flower: B5200, 772, Blanc

TECHNIQUES

- Buttonhole stitch (see page 74)
- Felt padding (see page 20)
- Long-and-short stitch natural shading (see page 64)
- Stem stitch (see page 74)
- Purl chippings (see page 31)
- Appliqué (see page 22)

TEMPLATES

See page 173

ORDER OF WORK

1 Transfer five petals and two leaves onto the fine calico using your chosen method. Make sure at least 2cm (¾in) is left between each element to give you space to cut them out later. Frame up with the calico backing.

2 For the leaves: cut two 15cm (6in) pieces of wire and couch these just inside the outside line of each leaf using one strand of 3364. Leave the tails of wire at the base of the leaves.

3 Using one strand of 3364 and beginning at the bottom edge, work buttonhole stitch over the wires. Work the stitches closely together.

4 Fill the leaves with one strand of 3363 using long-and-short stitch. The first row needs to go right up to but not over the buttonhole loops (over the wire).

5 Create a stem and veins on each leaf using one strand of 3364 and stem stitch.

6 Work the petals in the same way as the leaves. Use B5200 to couch the wire, create the buttonhole stitch and sew the first row of long-and-short stitch. Use Blanc to continue the long-and-short shading, and complete with a few stitches of 772 to highlight the centre of each of the petals.

7 Once the leaves and petals are complete, carefully cut out each of the elements as close to the buttonhole stitch as possible without cutting through them.

8 Build the flower on the background fabric. Draw the centre of the flower to start. Each leaf and petal is then attached separately. Attach the two leaves first: position each leaf then plunge the wires and sew into position behind the leaf, adding a few stitches to hold it in place at the base. Then add the petals, building to the foreground until all five petals are attached in the same way as the leaves.

9 Add two layers of felt padding to the centre of the flower. Apply a small piece of white fabric over the centre. Outline the flower centre with small gold wire check chippings. This will hide any stitches and joins that may be visible around the centre.

GOLDWORK & SILK SHADING COMBINED

Metal threads can enhance and bring another dimension to silk shading. Together they provide opulence and naturalism. Traditionally, goldwork and silk shading embroidery techniques were combined on ecclesiastical vestments and the garments of the very wealthy. Together they produce exquisite, colourful embroideries which draw one's eye with their beauty and elegance. Today, goldwork and silk shading are still mainly worked separately, but nevertheless when combined they can produce truly stunning pieces of embroidery.

A FEW BASIC RULES

1 Really, there is no limit to what you can do – your imagination and ability are all that restrict you. All the basic rules for both goldwork and silk shading apply when the two techniques are combined.

2 For a straightforward method of combination, larger areas can be worked in silk shading and then outlined and highlighted with goldwork using fine threads such as rococco, check threads and passings.

3 Traditionally, areas in which you wanted a more 'natural' look were worked in silk shading to give the most realistic effect. However, with the huge range of metal threads available now this does not have to be the case. Tones and shades are available in both mediums.

4 When considering your possible techniques think about what would suit each area and the design as a whole. Decide if you wish to include any padding and what medium would best cover this.

5 Consider the colours and textures you would like to see and also if you would like to add any three-dimensional elements.

6 Play with ideas, techniques and colours before you start to enable the most pleasing combination to be formed for your finished piece. Throughout this book, ideas worked in both mediums together and separately will give you inspiration for small and larger projects. Enjoy finding combinations that enhance your designs.

ORDER OF WORK

Generally, it is better to work silk shading before adding any gold or metal embellishment. This is for a number of reasons. The silk/cotton threads can easily catch on the metal threads and become damaged, and metal threads are not in danger of being damaged by constant work around them if worked last. Also, the correct weight (thickness) of goldwork embellishment can be more accurately chosen to highlight the silk shading; it is easy to add too strong an edge to an area and lose the delicacy of the silk shading.

For this project, see pages 80–81.

Complementary stitches

STEM STITCH

This stitch is good for lines and outlines. It can be worked in one row or multiple rows to add depth.

1 Bring the needle through the fabric at the start of the line to be worked.

2 Take the needle down through the fabric around 3mm (⅛in) away, slightly to the right of the line.

3 Bring the needle back up to the left of the first stitch, halfway along its length. Then take the needle down about 2mm (¹/₁₆in) ahead of the last stitch. Repeat until the desired length.

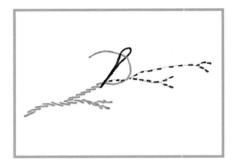 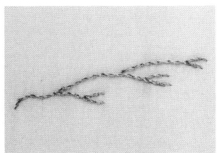 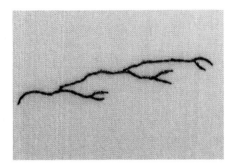

BUTTONHOLE STITCH

1 Bring the needle up through the fabric on the outer edge of the section. Insert the needle down in the section at a 90-degree angle, leaving a loop.

2 Come back up with the needle through the loop of the previous stitch, on the outer edge, gently pulling the thread flat. Repeat around the section. Keep the stitches close together so no fabric can be seen. If this is used for a three-dimensional element, work with one short and one long stitch alternately to strengthen the edge.

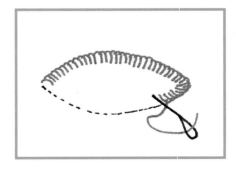 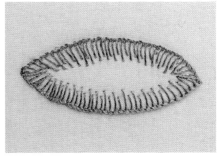 

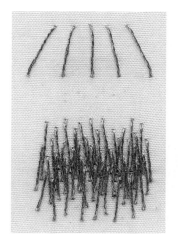
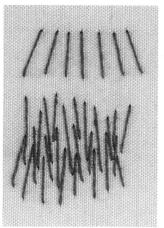

STRAIGHT STITCH

This is essentially creating single lines with the thread. Straight stitches can be used singly or placed in a random manner to give a fluffy effect.

1 Come up through the fabric and go down to form a stitch of the required length.

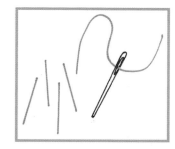

STACKED FLY STITCH

1 Mark a vein up the centre of the leaf. Place a straight stitch from the point to a little way down the central vein. Come out on the line to the side of the point and go down on the design line on the other side of the point, leaving the thread loose to form a loop.

2 Bring the needle back out on the centre line in the same hole as the first stitch, making sure that it is inside the loop. Take a small stitch over the thread on the vein line. Repeat the process, always coming up on the same side of the outline until the leaf is complete.

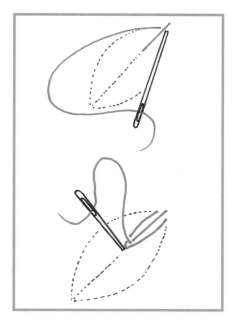

SATIN STITCH

Before working satin stitch, work a row of split stitch around the shape in order to form a boundary and slightly pad the edges. Work the satin stitch over the split stitch so that it completely covers it.

1 Make sure that the needle is always brought out on the same side of the design. Work straight stitches across the shape, keeping them parallel and even.

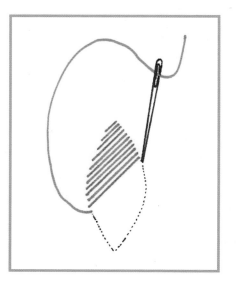

FRENCH KNOTS

For a larger knot, use a thicker thread or additional strands rather than making more wraps around the needle.

1 Fasten on a thread and bring it through to the front of the fabric. Place the needle under the thread and wrap the remaining thread around the needle twice. Take the needle down into the fabric almost through the same hole. Pull the thread up tidily around the base of the needle and pull the needle through to the wrong side of the fabric.

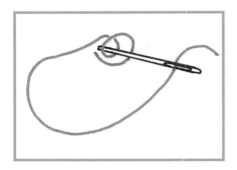
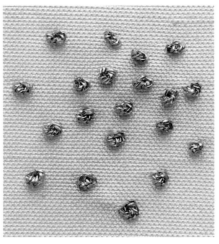
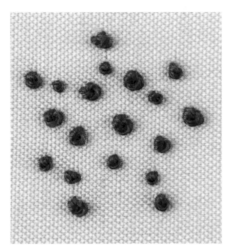

BULLION KNOTS

Use a longer length of thread than normal when working bullion knots as they require a lot of thread.

1 Bring the needle out through the fabric and take it back down a short distance away (this determines the length of the stitch). Leave the thread very loose.

2 Push the needle part of the way back through the fabric where it first came out. Carefully wind the thread around the needle point until the wrapping measures the length of the stitch.

3 Go back through the fabric at the opposite end of the stitch and carefully pull up the thread. If necessary, use the needle like a pulley to coax the thread through.

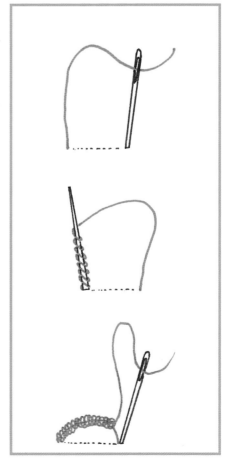

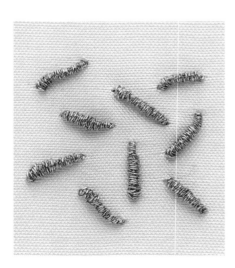
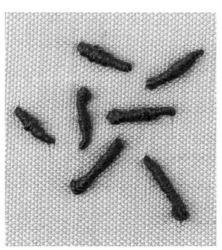

TWO-NEEDLE LEAF STITCH

1 Draw a line each side of the central vein. Fasten on a thread and make a stitch at the top of the central line going down on the point. Bring the same thread through the fabric a fraction below this stitch, coming up on one of the marked lines. Cross over the other marked line and go down on the edge, just below the point. Bring the needle up a little below the previous stitch on the marked line and leave the thread on the right-hand side of the leaf.

2 Fasten on a second thread and bring the needle out on the other marked line. Cross over the previous stitches to go down on the edge on the other side, just below the point. Bring the needle back up a fraction below the previous stitch, roughly level with the loose thread on the other side. Leaving this thread on the left-hand side, pick up the first thread again and repeat the process.

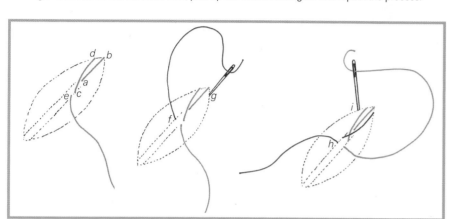

CHAIN STITCH

1 Bring the needle out through the fabric and take it back down almost in the same hole, leaving the thread loose.

2 Push the needle back up to create the required length of stitch, making sure it comes up inside the loop. Pull up on the thread to form the stitch and repeat as many times as necessary.

3 Finish with a stitch over the final loop. Individual chain stitches can be laid down in a random pattern and left plain or decorated with tiny purl chippings or a single straight stitch.

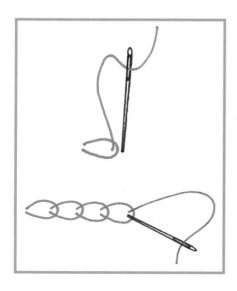

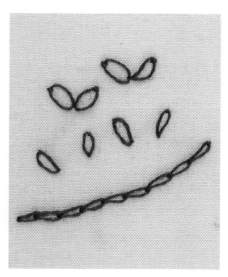

Combined Wild Rose

Hazel's design combining both goldwork and silk shading embroidery. Worked by student Kate Hedger.

FABRIC

- Cream silk dupion: 25 x 35cm (10 x 14in)
- Calico: 25 x 35cm (10 x 14in)

THREADS

- Gold heavy metal no. 30
- Gold Ophir
- No. 6 smooth passing: 1m (39in)
- Check thread no. 7: 1m (39in)
- Elizabethan twist: 3.5m (138in)
- Green 3-ply twist: 50cm (20in)
- Bright check purl no. 6: 20cm (8in)
- Smooth purl no. 6: 20cm (8in)
- DMC stranded cotton (use one strand unless otherwise stated): 3687, 3688, 3689, 819, 987

TECHNIQUES

- Long-and-short stitch natural shading (see page 64)
- Split stitch (see page 60)
- Satin stitch (see page 75)
- Purl chippings (see page 31)
- Couched threads (see pages 36–38)
- Twists (see page 39)
- Elizabethan twist (see page 46)

TEMPLATE

See page 174

ORDER OF WORK

Use gold heavy metal no. 30 to couch and sew all metal threads throughout. Use one strand of stranded cotton thread unless otherwise stated.

1 Transfer the design onto the silk dupion using your chosen method, marking single lines only for the stems. Frame up the fabric with the calico backing.

2 First add the stems – doing this now means it is easier to get a smooth flowing shape connecting the stems. Start with the long central stem, then add the other branch stems. Couch the green 3-ply twist with one waxed strand of 987, leaving 2.5cm (1in) tails at the beginning and end of each section to plunge when finished. When all the stems are complete, couch check thread no. 7 along the side marked with dotted lines using the gold heavy metal no. 30, again leaving 2.5cm (1in) tails at the start and end of each section. When all stems are sewn, take all tails down through the fabric and oversew behind the embroidery.

3 Now work all the silk-shaded areas. The buds are worked in a combination of 3688 and 3687. Firstly, split stitch around the outer edge in 3688. Fill in the bud with long-and-short natural shading, starting at the point and working towards the base using the two colours (see the direction diagram, right).

4 The petals on the main flower are worked next (refer to nos. 1–5 on the **4a** stitch order diagram, right). Use a combination of 3687, 3688, 3689 and 819. Each petal is worked in the same way: split stitch around the outer edge of petal no. 1 (not areas under other petals) in 819. Work a petal with natural-shaded long-and-short stitch, starting at the top point of the petal working to the centre in the four pinks (see the **4b** stitch direction diagram, right). Repeat for the other petals in order.

5 Using smooth passing no. 6, outline the main flower. Cut a 50cm (20in) length of passing and couch around the flower centre, leaving a 2.5cm (1in) tail at the beginning. When the centre is completely worked, take the passing through the fabric and bring up at the beginning of petal no. 1. Be very careful when taking this thread through the fabric so as not to damage any long-and-short stitches. Couch around the petal and then take the passing down and bring it up at petal no. 2. Complete the second petal no. 2 then repeat for petals no. 3 and 4 until the flower is completely outlined, leaving a 2.5cm (1in) tail. Take the tails of the passing down through the fabric and finish by oversewing behind the embroidery.

6 Couch the passing around the two buds in the same way.

7 Satin stitch the sepals for the buds in gold Ophir.

8 Work the leaves in Elizabethan twist in the diagonal method using waxed 987 to hold the thread in place. You can use single or doubled thread here (the sample is worked with a single thread).

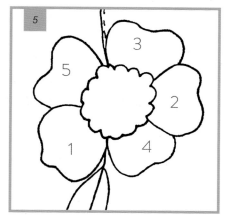

9 Fill in the centre of the flower with loopy chippings about 5mm (¼in) long in both bright check and smooth purls, randomly placed. You may find it helpful to have a stiletto handy to help these lay forming a true loop.

Combined Violet

Here you can see how Hazel's violet translates beautifully into different mediums. Using the whole design, this sample was worked by Jan and shows how well silk shading and goldwork go together.

FABRIC

- Gold/green silk dupion: 25 x 25cm (10 x 10in)
- Calico: 25 x 25cm (10 x 10in)

THREADS

Flowers
- DMC stranded cotton: 211, 210, 209, 208, 550
- Purple smooth passing no. 6: 50cm (20in)
- Gold smooth purl no. 8: 2cm (¾in)
- Invisible thread

Leaves
- DMC stranded cotton: 988, 987, 986, 936
- Green and gold fine 2-ply twist: 2m (79in)
- Gold heavy metal no. 30
- Leaf green wire check purl no. 8: 10cm (4in)

Stems and sepals
- Gold-green smooth passing no. 4 on green core: 2m (79in)

TECHNIQUES

- Split stitch (see page 60)
- Long-and-short stitch natural shading (see page 74)
- Elizabethan twist (see page 46)
- Couched threads (see pages 36–38)
- Purl chippings (see page 31)
- Chain stitch (see page 77)

TEMPLATE

See page 173

ORDER OF WORK

1 Transfer the design onto the silk dupion using your desired method, marking on all the lines. Frame up the fabric with the calico backing.

2 Work all the areas in stranded cotton first. Begin with the flowers and bud. Work from the background forward and use one strand of thread throughout. Work the petals in the same way as for the Silk Shaded Violet (see pages 68–69). To do this, first split stitch the outside edge of the petal in one strand of 211. Using single strands of stranded cottons 211, 210, 209, 208 and 550, add long-and-short stitch natural shading to each petal. When the flowers are complete, work the bud in the same way.

3 Next, work the top sides of the leaves with turnovers in the same way as for the Silk Shaded Violet (see pages 68–69). Split stitch around the outside of the under section using one strand of 988. Complete the under section with long-and-short stitch natural shading using single strands of 988, 987 and 986.

4 For the turnover of the leaves and the main leaf, work in fine green metallic twist tied down with gold heavy metal no. 30. Embroider each section using the Elizabethan twist traditional method (see page 46). Do not forget to leave 2.5cm (1in) tails at the start and finish of each section when working either the Elizabethan twist method or couched passing, for plunging and finishing off behind the work.

5 Outline the sepals with gold-green smooth passing no. 4 couched in gold heavy metal no. 30. Plunge and sew back each tail. Fill each sepal segment with long chips of leaf green no. 8 wire check purl to form a satin stitch with the chips.

6 Outline the bud and each of the individual petals in purple passing no. 6 couched down with invisible thread. Plunge and oversew back all the tails.

7 Fill the flower centre with tiny chips of gold smooth purl no. 8.

8 Outline the leaves in the gold-green smooth passing no. 4, couched down with gold heavy metal no. 30 and plunge the tails. Oversew the tails on the reverse of the embroidery.

9 For the stems, couch one strand of gold-green passing no. 4 with gold heavy metal no. 30 for the flower stems. Use two strands of the gold-green passing no. 4 couched for the leaf stems. Plunge the tails and oversew to the back. I worked the stems near the end of this piece as they seemed to sit better when worked after the larger sections.

10 For the small leaves on the flower stems use two strands of 936. Work two detached chain stitches either side of the stem to form the outside of each pair of leaves. Add a straight stitch to complete the centres.

Combined 3D Christmas Rose

Designed by Hazel; worked by Jan.

ADDING A THREE-DIMENSIONAL ELEMENT

Using the techniques described in goldwork and silk shading (see pages 25–55 and 57–71) there are many different ways to add a three-dimensional element. The basic techniques will stay the same and within that you can do whatever you would like. Mix and match techniques, but do just check the weight balance of the various different elements.

FABRIC

- Fine calico, two pieces: 30 x 30cm (12 x 12in)
- Red silk dupion: 30 x 30cm (12 x 12in)
- Yellow felt: 5 x 5cm (2 x 2in)

THREADS

- DMC stranded cotton: Blanc, 3865, 3013, 987
- Silver check thread no. 7: 75cm (29½in)
- Silver heavy metal no. 30
- Gold heavy metal no. 30
- Gold bright check purl no. 8: 20cm (8in)
- Fine wire: 105cm (41½in)

TECHNIQUES

- Felt padding (see page 20)
- Buttonhole stitch (see page 74)
- Purl chippings (see page 31)
- Long-and-short stitch natural shading (see page 64)
- Couched threads (see pages 36–38)
- Stacked fly stitch (see page 75)

TEMPLATE

See page 173

ORDER OF WORK

1 Mark the flower centre and the two leaves onto the silk fabric using your desired method. Frame up with one piece of calico for the backing. Pad the centre circle with two layers of yellow felt.

2 Mark five petals onto the other piece of calico, making sure there is a 2cm (¾in) gap between each petal. Frame up.

3 Work the leaves using two strands of 987 in stacked fly stitch.

4 For the petals, cut a 15cm (6in) length of wire and couch this just inside the outside line of each petal using one strand of Blanc; leave 2.5cm (1in) tails of wire at the base of the petal.

5 Using one strand of Blanc and beginning at the bottom edge, work buttonhole stitch over the wire, packed closely together, with the loops on the outside of the petal. Make the stitches of varying length for strength.

6 Work each petal in long-and-short stitch natural shading, using single strands of Blanc with 3865 and 3013 for highlights. Start at the point of the petal and work towards the base (which will be next to the centre). When all petals are complete, cut each one out very carefully, as close to the buttonhole loops as possible. (Be very careful not to cut the thread.)

7 Outline around the edge of the petals with an oversewn row of silver check thread no. 7, stitched with silver heavy metal no. 30. Leave 2.5cm (1in) tails to plunge when putting the flower together.

8 Build the flower on the main fabric, carefully positioning each petal. Plunge the wire and check thread no. 7 through the fabric and sew in place behind. Finish with tiny stitches, oversewing the base of the petals in place. Fill the centre of the flower with small chips of gold bright check purl no. 8 attached with gold heavy metal no. 30.

Flowers

One of Hazel's favourite places was her garden and she loved flowers; many pieces of work that she designed included flowers. In fact, she had so many flower designs that the whole book could have been just flowers! Flowers can be embroidered in many ways using fine coloured metallic threads, silk shading and by adding embellishment. They can also be large, standalone designs or small and part of an overall picture. This section looks at mixing all these together and the different effects this can create. Treat this section like a directory of techniques and ideas for you to use, build on and experiment with to achieve your desired finish and your own style.

For this project, see pages 96–98.

Flowers Sampler

Designed by Hazel; worked by Jan. Note that several of the flowers incorporate 371 thread, which is a goldwork thread that has a cotton core wrapped in metal; for this reason, 2.5cm (1in) long tails need to be left at the start and end of each thread for plunging (see page 43).

SAMPLER KEY

1. Tulip no. 1
2. Spider chrysanthemums no. 1
3. Clematis
4. Spider chrysanthemums no. 2
5. Tulip no. 2
6. Lavender
7. Crocus no. 1
8. Forget-me-nots
9. Crocus no. 2
10. Hyacinth
11. Coreopsis
12. Petunia
13. Daisy no. 1
14. Buddleia no. 1
15. Hollyhock
16. Buddleia no. 2
17. Daisy no. 2
18. Roses no. 1
19. Pansy no. 1
20. Pansy no. 2
21. Roses no. 2
22. Carnation no. 1
23. Daffodils
24. Sunflower
25. Cornflowers
26. Carnation no. 2

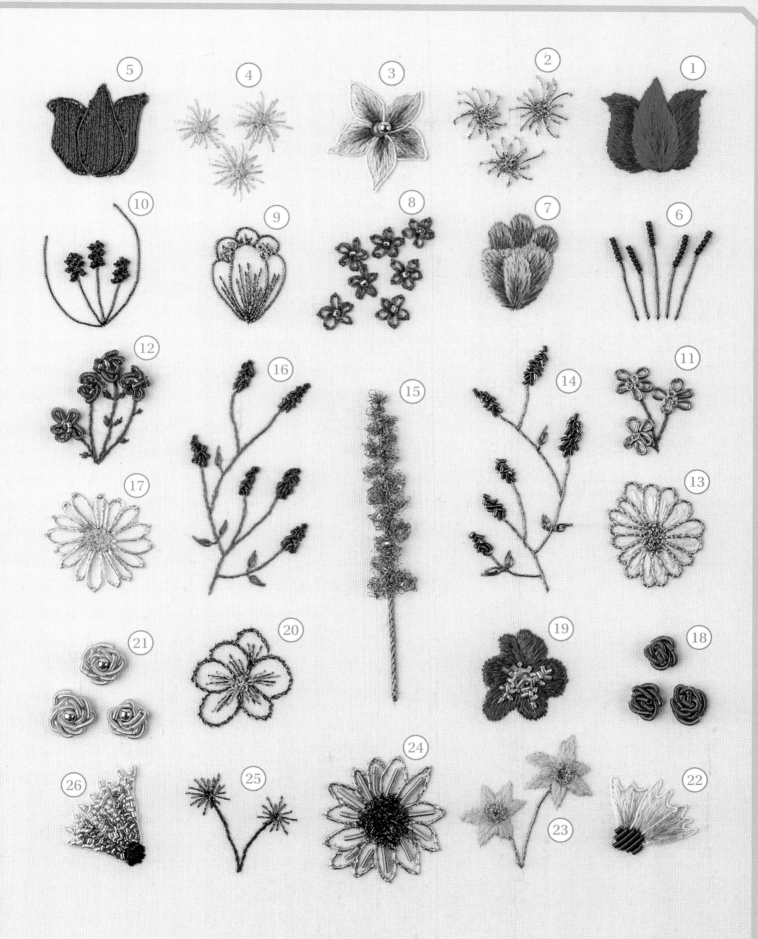

FABRIC

- Ivory silk: 40 x 40cm (16 x 16in)
- Calico: 40 x 40cm (16 x 16in)

THREADS & TECHNIQUES

- See each individual flower description

TEMPLATE

See page 174

ORDER OF WORK

1 Transfer the design onto the fabric using your chosen method, taking care only to mark areas that will be covered by the embroidery. For example, for the spider chrysanthemums, only mark the centre as the petals are very fine and will be worked freehand. If there is a stem, only add the central line.

2 Frame up with the calico backing.

3 For this particular piece I started from the top row, working from right to left (if you are left handed you may need to work from left to right), and then continued going down the rows in order. As I am right-handed my left hand is above the work. This reduced the risk of damaging work already completed.

1. TULIP NO. 1

THREADS

- DMC stranded cotton (use one strand throughout): 816, 321, 666

1 Split stitch around the outside edges of the back two petals in 816. Using long-and-short stitch natural shading, work 816 around the edges and 321 where the petals touch the front petal. Start at the points and work to the centre.

2 Split stitch around the front petal in 666.

3 Use long-and-short stitch natural shading mainly in 666, with 816 as a highlight, towards the centre of the front petal.

2. SPIDER CHRYSANTHEMUMS NO. 1

THREADS

- Light and medium pink 371 thread
- Gold smooth purl no. 8
- Gold heavy metal no. 30

1 Work straight stitches in pink 371 thread, with the two shades spiralling out from the centre. Come up near the centre and go down away from the centre each time for consistency. Keep the stitches loose to give shape.

2 For the flower centre, use fuzzy effect in gold purl stitched down with gold heavy metal no. 30.

3. CLEMATIS

THREADS

- DMC stranded cotton (use one strand throughout): 208, 209, 210, 211
- White opal 371 thread
- Invisible thread
- Gold sequin and bead

1 Work each petal individually, working from the back forward. Split stitch around the outer edge of the petal.

2 Fill in the petal using natural long-and-short stitch natural shading in all four shades.

3 Outline each petal with white opal 371 thread couched with invisible thread. Add a sequin and bead for the centre.

4. SPIDER CHRYSANTHEMUMS NO. 2

THREADS

- DMC stranded cotton
  (use one strand throughout):
  3689, 3727, 725

1 Work loose straight stitches from the centre of the flower outwards in 3689 and 3727. Keep the stitches loose to give shape.

2 Create the centre in French knots using one strand of 725.

5. TULIP NO. 2

THREADS

- Red 371 thread
- DMC Light Effects E815
- Invisible thread

1 Edge the petals with red 371 thread couched with invisible thread, leaving 2.5cm (1in) tails at the start and finish. One continuous length can be used, plunging and bringing back through where necessary: start with the front petal and then work the back two. Plunge the tails and oversew to the back of the flower.

2 Fill each petal in satin stitch worked vertically using one strand of E815.

6. LAVENDER

THREADS

- Dark green 371 thread
- Purple wire check purl no. 8
- Invisible thread

1 Leaving 2.5cm (1in) tails at the start and finish, couch the dark green 371 thread up each stem with invisible thread. Use one continuous piece of thread, coming up at the base of the stem each time. Plunge the tails and oversew to the back.

2 For each flowerhead, add a long purple wire check purl chip above the stem attached with invisible thread.

7. CROCUS NO. 1

THREADS

- DMC stranded cotton
  (use one strand throughout):
  209, 208, 210, 725

1 Work each petal in the same way. Working from the background forwards, split stitch around the outer edge in 209.

2 Fill each petal using long-and-short stitch natural shading, using a combination of 208, 209 and 210, shading where appropriate.

3 Complete the flower by adding French knots worked in 725.

8. FORGET-ME-NOTS

THREADS

- DMC stranded cotton: 798
- Gold beads

1 Work five single chain stitches radiating from each centre in two strands of 798 to form the petals.

2 Add a gold bead to each flower for its centre.

9. CROCUS NO. 2

THREADS

- Purple 371 thread
- DMC metallic E3837
- Gold Ophir
- Invisible thread

1 Leaving 2.5cm (1in) tails at the start and finish, edge the petals in purple 371 thread, couched down with invisible thread. Use one continuous length, plunging and coming up through the fabric where necessary. Plunge the tails and oversew to the back.

2 Add a number of straight stitches to the centre of each petal in E3837, using one strand to add definition and colour.

3 Complete by adding French knots in gold Ophir for the stamens.

10. HYACINTH

THREADS

- Green 371 thread
- Purple wire check purl
- Invisible thread

1 Couch green 371 with invisible thread along the stems and leaves, leaving 2.5cm (1in) tails at the start and finish. Start at the base and work up each time. Plunge the tails and oversew to the back.

2 Attach small chips in purple wire check purl for the flowerheads, laying them haphazardly.

11. COREOPSIS

THREADS

- DMC stranded cotton: 909
- Gold smooth purl no. 8
- Gold heavy metal no. 30
- Gold Ophir

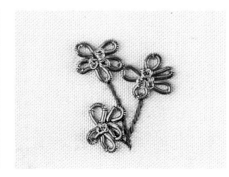

1 With one strand of 909, stem stitch the stems.

2 For the petals, use gold smooth purl no. 8 cut into 6mm (¼in) lengths. Use each length to form a loop from the centre of the flower and tie down with gold heavy metal no. 30 like a chain stitch. Add five of these for each flower.

3 Work French knots in gold Ophir to form the flower centres.

12. PETUNIA

THREADS

- DMC stranded cotton: 909
- Dark pink rough purl
- Gold smooth purl no. 8

1 Using one strand of dark green 909, stem stitch the stems. Add the leaves in 909, working in satin stitch.

2 For the petals, use dark pink rough purl cut into 6mm (¼in) lengths. Use each length to form a loop from the centre of the flower, but do not tie down. Add five of these for each flower.

3 Add a chip in gold smooth purl no. 8 to the centre to finish; a good alternative would be a gold bead.

13. DAISY NO. 1

THREADS

- Silver superfine rococco
- Silver heavy metal no. 30
- Gold smooth purl no. 8
- Gold heavy metal no. 30
- DMC stranded cotton: Blanc, 3865

1 Couch silver superfine rococco around each petal, secured with silver heavy metal no. 30. Use one continuous thread, plunging and bringing up where required.

2 Add a section of long-and-short stitch natural shading in Blanc and 3865 (one strand) to each petal, coming out from the centre of the flower. Do not completely fill the petals.

3 Embroider the centre with tiny chips of gold smooth purl, attached with gold heavy metal no. 30.

14. BUDDLEIA NO. 1

THREADS

- Light green 371 thread
- Dark purple smooth purl
- Dark purple rough purl
- Invisible thread

1 Couch light green 371 thread with invisible thread for stems. Use one continuous thread.

2 Still using the green 371 thread, create each leaf with a single chain stitch. Start at the point of the leaf and tie the loop down at the stem. Add a straight line down the centre of the leaf in the green 371 thread.

3 To form the flowers, use the two types of purple purls. Cut tiny chips and attach to the top of the stems in a haphazard formation.

15. HOLLYHOCK

THREADS

- Light green 3-ply twist
- Pink rough purl
- Invisible thread
- Gold beads

1 To form the stem, couch down the light green 3-ply twist using invisible thread.

2 Add the flowers to the stem using the fuzzy effect (see page 32). Add each flower individually and gently cup it to make it three-dimensional using pink rough purl.

3 Add small gold beads for the centres.

16. BUDDLEIA NO. 2

THREADS

- DMC stranded cotton:
  701, 327, 3740

1 Form the stems using stem stitch and one strand of 701.

2 Create leaves in 701 with a chain stitch, tying down at the stems; add a straight stitch down the centre.

3 Form the flowers with a mixture of bullion knots and French knots in 327 and 3740.

17. DAISY NO. 2

THREADS

- Silver Ophir
- DMC stranded cotton: 725, 973

1 Work each petal as an individual chain stitch in silver Ophir.

2 Fill the flower centre with French knots in 725 and 973.

18. ROSES NO. 1

THREADS

- Rose red rough purl
- Invisible thread

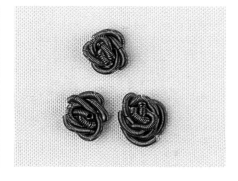

1 Cut the rose red rough purl into lengths of 3–6mm (1/8–1/4in). Using invisible thread to stitch the purls down, take each individual length of purl and form interlinking loops to create a rosette. Start in the centre of the flower and work in a spiral formation outwards, linking each purl chip to the previous one.

19. PANSY NO. 1

THREADS

- DMC stranded cotton (use one strand throughout): 208, 552
- Gold smooth purl no. 8
- Gold heavy metal no. 30

1 Work each petal in the same way. Split stitch around the edge of each petal in 208.

2 Using long-and-short stitch natural shading, embroider each petal in 552 and 208, leaving a central line empty from the centre of the flower.

3 Using gold purl, add tiny chippings to the empty section of each petal. Using gold purl, add loops about 6mm (1/4in) long to the centre. Secure these with gold heavy metal no. 30.

20. PANSY NO. 2

THREADS

- DMC Jewel Effects
  (use one strand throughout):
  E3837, E5282

1 Stem stitch around each petal in E3837.

2 To complete each petal, add straight stitch colour highlights from the centre out using E3837 and E5282.

3 Finish the flower centres with French knots using E5282.

21. ROSES NO. 2

THREADS

- Old gold rough purl
- Gold heavy metal no. 30
- Gold beads

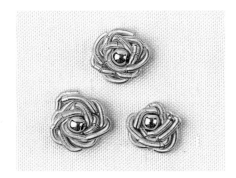

1 Attach a gold bead to centre of each flower using gold heavy metal no. 30.

2 Cut the old gold rough purl into 6mm (¼in) lengths. Stem stitch at least two rows around the bead using the cut lengths of rough purl.

22. CARNATION NO. 1

THREADS

- DMC stranded cotton:
  899, 3326, 818
- White opal 371 thread
- Dark green rough purl
- Invisible thread

1 With long-and-short stitch natural shading, infill the petals using single strands of 899, 3326 and 818, working the outer back petals first; there is no need to split stitch first.

2 Outline each petal in white opal 371 stitched down with invisible thread.

3 Form the sepals with dark green rough purl using long chips cut to the right length, attached with invisible thread.

23. DAFFODILS

THREADS

- DMC stranded cotton
  (use one strand throughout):
  307, 444
- Green 371 thread
- Gold smooth purl no. 8
- Invisible thread

1 Leaving 2.5cm (1in) tails at the start and end, couch green 371 thread with invisible thread to form the stems. Plunge the tails and oversew at the back.

2 Split stitch around the petals using 307. Shade each petal with long-and-short stitch in 307 and 444.

3 Create the centre with fuzzy effect in smooth purl no. 8. Form small balls then place a pencil in the centre and mould the ball around it to form a tubular effect. Stitch in place with invisible thread in the centre of the tube.

24. SUNFLOWER

THREADS

- Gold passing no. 4
- Gold heavy metal no. 30
- Gold smooth purl
- Brown rough purl
- Invisible thread

1 Leaving 2.5cm (1in) tails at the start and end, couch the gold passing with gold heavy metal no. 30 around each of the petals in one continuous length. Take the passing down through the fabric at the end of each petal and bring it back up to the front of the fabric at the start of the next petal until all have been outlined. Then plunge the start and end tails and sew back behind the embroidery.

2 Add a long chip of gold smooth purl to the centre of each petal, coming out from the centre.

3 Fuzzy effect the centre of the flower (see page 32) in brown rough purl stitched down with invisible thread.

25. CORNFLOWERS

THREADS

- DMC stranded cotton: 895
- DMC Jewel Effects: E3843

1 Using 895, stem stitch both stems.

2 With straight stitches in E3843, form the flower with straight stitches radiating from the flower centres.

26. CARNATION NO. 2

THREADS

- White opal 371 thread
- Dark pink smooth purl
- Light pink smooth purl
- Silver smooth purl no. 8
- DMC stranded cotton: 895
- Invisible thread

1 Outline the petals with white opal 371 couched down with invisible thread.

2 Split stitch around the outside of the sepals cup and then cover in satin stitch worked in one strand of 895.

3 Using very small chips of dark pink, light pink and silver purl, fill the petals, shading as appropriate.

For the templates. see page 174.

Couch silver check thread around the edge of each petal. Fill each petal with contour couched white opal 371 thread. Add small gold beads for the flower centre.

Couch silver fine rococco around each petal. Add three straight stitches to each petal in silver Ophir. Using smooth gold purl no. 8, complete the centre of the flower using the fuzzy effect technique.

Flower: outline with a line of couched gold check thread no. 7 and smooth passing. Fill the centre with very small pink wire check purl chippings.

Leaves: outline with gold over-stretched pearl purl with a line inside of normal pearl purl. Add a smattering of small green wire purl chips.

Stem: couch gold Grecian twist.

Outline with couched 3-ply twist.
Vein in couched green 371 thread.

Work in Elizabethan twist worked in the traditional method tied down with DMC stranded cotton 470.

Outline and add the central vein with couched gold check thread no. 7.

Complete with cutwork of green wire check purl and rough purl.

EXPLORING A SIMPLE FLOWER IN STRANDED COTTON

For the templates. see page 174.

Split stitch around each petal in DMC Blanc. Complete each petal in long-and-short stitch, using DMC stranded cotton Blanc, 746 and B5200. Add gold beads for the centre.

Couch four strands of DMC Blanc with one strand to form the outline of each petal. Add three straight stitches in DMC 746 in the centre of each petal. Satin stitch the centre of the flower using two strands of DMC 725.

Flower: split stitch around each petal in DMC B5200. Satin stitch each petal in two strands of DMC B5200. Complete the centre in French knots worked in DMC 3727 and 316.

Leaves: split stitch around each leaf in DMC 470. Long-and-short stitch shade the leaves in natural shading in DMC 470, 471 and 472.

Stem: couch on a cord made from four strands of DMC 470.

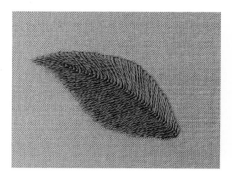

Using two strands of DMC 470, work the leaf in stacked fly stitch.

Outline with a six-stranded cord of DMC 470 couched into position. Add the vein using two strands of DMC 470 and embroider in stem stitch.

Split stitch around the edge of the leaf in DMC 469. Use natural long-and-short stitch to shade the leaf using DMC 469, 470, 471 and 472.

Gold and Silkwork Iris

Hazel designed this to combine the beauty of nature with the whole range of gold, silk shading and three-dimensional techniques. In this piece, each technique embellishes, while enhancing nature and looking its best. Worked by Jan.

FABRIC

- Pale green silk dupion: 40 x 40cm (16 x 16in)
- Calico: 40 x 40cm (16 x 16in) and 20 x 20cm (8 x 8in)
- White felt: 15 x 15cm (6 x 6in)

THREADS

- DMC stranded cotton: 838, 801, 300, 727, 726, 746
- Gold 3-ply twist: 1m (39in)
- Gold superfine pearl purl: 75cm (29½in)
- Gold bright check purl no. 6: 1.5m (59in)
- Gold rough purl no. 6: 1.5m (59in)
- Gold check thread no. 7: 1m (39in)
- Yellow bump/soft cotton
- Yellow Gütermann thread
- Gold Ophir
- Gold heavy metal no. 30
- Fine wire: 50cm (20in)

TECHNIQUES

- Long-and-short stitch natural shading (see page 64)
- Split stitch (see page 60)
- Felt padding (see page 20)
- Couched threads & Twist (see pages 36–39)
- Bump/soft cotton padding (see page 21)
- Purl chippings (see page 31)
- Graded cutwork (see page 33)
- Buttonhole stitch (see page 74)

TEMPLATES

See page 175

ORDER OF WORK

1 Transfer the main design onto the silk using your desired method, then transfer the three additional three-dimensional petals onto the smaller piece of calico. Frame up both, with the larger calico piece backing the main design.

2 On the main design, start with the padding; attach all of these with Gütermann thread: pad the top back petal with one layer of felt. Pad the two side petals with two layers of felt. Pad the bud with three layers of felt. Pad the three leaves with soft cotton. Taper off the padding at each end, cutting the threads away from underneath to give a smooth effect.

3 Split stitch around the background petals using one strand of 838 and then embroider with long-and-short stitch natural shading. Only work over the top and main body of the petals as the three dimensional petals will cover quite a lot. Do this using single strands of 838, 801, 300, 727, 726 and 746 as required to give the natural flow of each petal.

4 On the two side petals, form a line in split stitch using the gold rough purl. Cut each length to approximately 5mm (¼in). This forms the central stamen.

5 Outline all three petals with gold check thread no. 7 couched down with gold heavy metal no. 30, leaving 2.5cm (1in) tails at the start and finish to be taken through to the back of the work and oversewn in place.

6 Outline the leaves, stem and bud with gold superfine pearl purl couched in gold heavy metal no. 30. On the bud add pearl purl in sections to create the idea of depth (see diagram, above right).

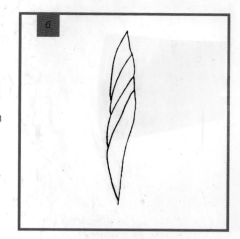

7 Fill the top section of the bud using single strands of 838 and 801 stranded cotton, in long-and-short stitch. Satin stitch each of the other sections using gold Ophir.

8 Couch gold 3-ply twist inside the superfine pearl purl for the stem with gold heavy metal no. 30, making sure the rows lie closely together, paying particular attention to the bottom half as this is most visible. Plunge and tie back all the tails.

9 All the leaves are worked in cutwork. Each length of metal needs to be measured before it is attached. To do this, lay the metal over the soft cotton, matching it to the pearl purl edge. Dent the end with your needle and then cut. Attach with either waxed Gütermann or gold heavy metal no. 30. Try to always come up on the same side.

10 Refer to the stitch-order diagram, right. Work the right-hand leaf (no. 1) first using two pieces of bright check purl no. 6, then one of rough purl no. 6 and repeat. Try to keep a long angle to help when the leaf narrows; work bottom left to top right. Work the left-hand leaf (no. 2) next, using just rough purl no. 6, working in the opposite direction: bottom right to top left. Work the central leaf (no. 3), using just bright check no. 6 throughout, bottom right to top left.

11 Now turn your attention to the three three-dimensional petals on the smaller piece of calico fabric. Couch wire just inside the edges of the outline using one strand of 838, spacing the stitches approximately 2mm (1⁄16in) apart. Cross over the wires at the lower edge, couching them together so that there is a long end of 2.5cm (1in) left at each corner (see diagrams below right).

12 Work buttonhole stitch around the edge of each petal using one strand of 838. Start at the base between the two wires and work right around the petal.

13 Complete each petal using long-and-short stitch natural shading; work the long-and-short stitch into the buttonhole loops but not over them. Use single strands of 838, 801, 300, 727, 726 and 746, shading where appropriate.

14 On petal no. 1, add a row of stem stitch in rough purl no. 6 to the centre to form the stamen.

15 When all the petals are complete, carefully cut out as close to the buttonhole stitch as possible. It is best to do this in stages so as not to cut any stitches. Do not cut the wires as these are used to attach the petals.

16 Oversew gold check thread no. 7 around the edge of each petal using gold heavy metal no. 30, leaving a 2.5cm (1in) tail at the start and finish.

17 Position the three three-dimensional petals in place and plunge the wire and check thread no. 7 tails through to the wrong side of the embroidery. Oversew them in place behind the embroidery.

18 Using very small stitches in 838, oversew the central edges of the petals down to the main piece of embroidery.

19 Complete the embroidery by filling the centre of the flower with loops of rough purl no. 6. Cut the purl about 1cm (1⁄2in) long and stitch each piece into a loop in irregular directions to form the 'bearded' effect. To finish, gently mould the three-dimensional petals into position.

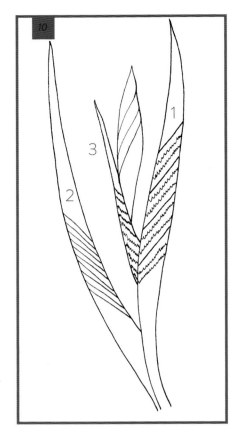

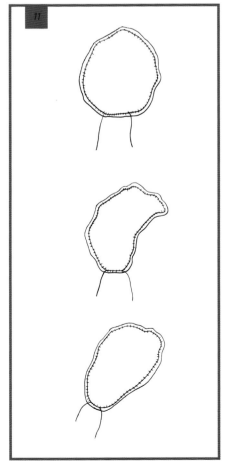

98

Trees

Trees are beautiful structures that lend themselves to embroidery. Metallic threads are perfect for trees as they provide texture and easily simulate the natural formations of bark and leaves, while highlights of silk shading in foliage make for beautiful and realistic images. This section has both small trees that can be used in relief and larger trees that can be added to the foreground of a landscape or embroidered as examples on their own.

For this project, see pages 106–107.

Trees Sampler

Designed and worked by Jan.

SAMPLER KEY

1. Round
2. Columnar
3. Conical
4. Low branched
5. Horizontally branched
6. Prostate
7. Round headed
8. Pyramidal
9. Open

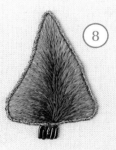

FABRIC

- Ivory silk: 40 x 40cm (16 x 16in)
- Calico: 40 x 40cm (16 x 16in)

THREADS & TECHNIQUES

- See each individual tree description. This sampler gives examples of tree shapes and different methods to highlight shape and texture, not specific species.

TEMPLATE

See page 176

ORDER OF WORK

1 Transfer the design onto the fabric using your desired method, taking care only to mark areas that will be covered by the embroidery.

2 Frame up with the calico backing.

3 For this particular piece I started on the top row then worked from the right on the second row towards the left. I continued in this way, going down a row each time, working right to left. As I am right-handed my left hand is above the work. This meant there was little chance I could damage work already completed. (If you are left-handed, you will need to work from left to right.)

1. ROUND

THREADS

- DMC stranded cotton: 319, 989, 3031
- Dark green and Christmas green rough purl
- Invisible thread

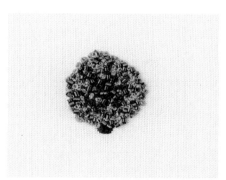

1 Randomly place French knots over the tree canopy using one strand of 989 towards the edge and 319 in the centre, leaving small gaps.

2 Fill the gaps with tiny chips stitched down with invisible thread – use Christmas green purl towards the edge and dark green purl in the centre. This gives a lovely highlight.

3 Using two strands of 3031, satin stitch the trunk.

2. COLUMNAR

THREADS

- DMC Light Effects: 5279
- Mint chocolate chip 371 thread

1 Work the canopy in stacked fly stitch using the 371 thread.

2 Vertically satin stitch the trunk using one strand of Light Effects 5279.

3. CONICAL

THREADS

- DMC stranded cotton (use one strand throughout): 890, 561, 562, 433

1 Work irregular, random fly stitches in 890, 562 and 561, starting with 890 and building up layers of 561 and 562 to add depth and shade. Be careful not to overfill.

2 Vertically satin stitch the trunk using 433.

4. LOW BRANCHED

THREADS

- DMC stranded cotton
  (use one strand throughout):
  699, 701, 702, 703, 938

1 For the trunk, embroider three bullion knots in a vertical direction next to each other using 938.

2 For the leaves, embroider irregular straight stitches: start with a first layer of 699 then add a layer of 701, 702 and 703. Be careful to position the lighter colours to accentuate depth.

5. HORIZONTALLY BRANCHED

THREADS

- DMC stranded cotton
  (use one strand throughout):
  3348, 3347, 3346, 3345
- Brown passing
- Invisible thread

1 Outline the canopy in split stitch using 3348.

2 Embroider the canopy in long-and-short stitch tapestry shading, shading where appropriate. Use all the colours described, from 3345 through to 3348.

3 Leaving 2.5cm (1in) tails at the start and end, work the trunk in continuous vertical rows of brown passing couched with invisible thread. Plunge the tails then oversew to the back.

6. PROSTRATE

THREADS

- Lime green 371 thread
- Grass green 371 thread
- Emerald green 371 thread
- Brown wire check purl
- Invisible thread

1 Attach a small horizontal brown chip for the trunk, stitched down with invisible thread.

2 For the canopy, embroider irregular horizontal straight stitches in 371 thread, starting with emerald green then building up with grass green. Use lime green for highlights.

7. ROUND HEADED

THREADS

- DMC stranded cotton
  (use one strand throughout):
  3371, 3031, 3021
- Lime green 371 thread
- Grass green 371 thread
- Emerald green 371 thread
- Invisible thread

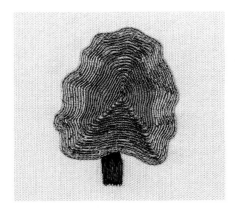

1 Embroider the trunk in long-and-short stitch tapestry shading using 3371, 3031 and 3021. Shade where appropriate. (Rows of stem stitch could also be used here.)

2 For the canopy, couch rows of continuous 371 thread with invisible thread: start at the edge with lime green, then after three rows change to grass green and finally, after seven rows, change to emerald green.Remember to leave 2.5cm (1in) tails at the start and end to plunge.

8. PYRAMIDAL

THREADS

- DMC stranded cotton (use one strand throughout): 703, 702, 701, 699
- Lime green 3-ply twist
- Brown wire check purl
- Invisible thread

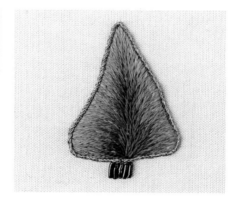

1 Split stitch around the canopy using 701.

2 Embroider the canopy in long-and-short natural shading using the full range of greens, from 703 to 699. Shade where appropriate.

3 Outline the canopy in lime green 3-ply twist couched down with invisible thread, leaving 2.5cm (1in) tails at the start and end. Plunge all tails and oversew behind the embroidery.

4 Add long vertical chips to form the trunk using brown wire check purl.

9. OPEN

THREADS

- DMC stranded cotton (use one strand throughout): 3031, 3021
- Grass green smooth purl
- Emerald green smooth purl
- Invisible thread

1 For the trunk, embroider compact rows of stem stitch, using 3021 as a highlight and 3031 as the shading.

2 For the leaves, embroider using the fuzzy effect. Make the leaf balls using both grass green and emerald green smooth purl, secured with invisible thread.

Small Trees

For the templates, see page 177.

WISTERIA

THREADS

- DMC stranded cotton: 470, 208
- DMC Jewel Effects 5289
- Burnished gold and brown 371 threads
- Invisible thread
- Purple wire check purl

1 Start with the two top centre branches. Couch down burnished gold with invisible thread: work from the branch ends down the centre of the trunk. Then add the brown with the burnished gold and work each branch down through the trunk, working from the centre out – twist them occasionally to add texture. Fill any gaps at the base of the trunk. Remember to leave 2.5cm (1in) threads at each end and, once the couching is complete, plunge all ends and tie back.

2 Use one strand of 470 throughout for the foliage. Work a short stem in stem stitch, add a detached chain stitch at the end of each stem and then add pairs of detached chain stitches along the stem.

3 Embroider flowers hanging down from the branches using bullion knots in a combination of two strands: one strand of 208 and one strand of 5289 to give a shimmer effect. Then add long purple wire check chips secured with invisible thread as highlights. Fill the branches.

CORYLUS 'CONTORTA' (CORKSCREW HAZEL)

THREADS

- Brown 3-ply twist
- Gold wire check purl
- Invisible thread

1 For the trunk, couch brown 3-ply twist with invisible thread, leaving 2.5cm (1in) tails at the start and end. Use a separate length for each trunk and tie back the plunged ends carefully behind the trunk on the wrong side once the trunks are complete.

2 For the catkins, cut approximately 3–6mm (⅛–¼in) lengths of gold wire check purl and stitch into place, grouping in two or three lengths, on various parts of the trunk to your requirements.

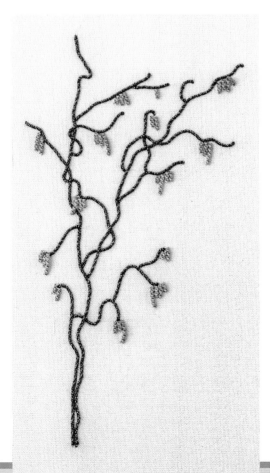

HAWTHORN

THREADS

- DMC stranded cotton (use one strand throughout): 938, 433, 3350, 3687, 3688
- Lime green rough purl
- Invisible thread

1 For the trunk, use 938 and 433 to build up rows of stem stitch, working from the end of the branch down through the trunk. Closely pack the stitches together and shade where appropriate.

2 For the leaves, add a very fine layer of fuzzy effect in lime green purl tied down with invisible thread along all the branches.

3 Using 3350, 3687 and 3688, work French knots haphazardly, spacing them out to create natural-looking flowers along the branches.

FIR TREE

THREADS

- DMC stranded cotton (use one strand throughout): 3371, 3031, 3021 (browns), 3345, 3346, 3347 (greens)

1 Split stitch the sides of the trunk using 303.

2 Embroider the trunk in long-and-short stitch tapestry shading using 3371, 3031 and 3021.

3 Complete the leaves in detached fly stitch. Build them up gradually in layers using 3345, 3346 and 3347; start with 3345 as the base and use 3347 topmost to highlight. Pack them closely together to form the fir needles.

WILLOW

THREADS

- DMC stranded cotton: 989, 988
- Green 371 thread
- Brown 3-ply twist
- Invisible thread

1 For the trunk, couch 3-ply brown twist 3 in rows closely packed together using invisible thread. Start at the end of each branch and work down through the trunk, working right to left. Remember to leave 2.5cm (1in) tails at the start and end, then plunge all ends and carefully tie back behind the embroidery once the couching is complete.

2 Using two strands of 989 and 988, work overlapping straight stitches for each of the leaf fronds. Highlight with straight stitches in green 371 thread.

Bonsai Tree

Hazel loved to work personal pieces for people and this Bonsai tree was
one of those: a special piece for a special person.

FABRIC

- Cream silk dupion: 35 x 20cm
  (14 x 8in)
- Brown silk dupion: 10 x 20cm
  (4 x 8in)
- Grey silk dupion: 10 x 10cm
  (4 x 4in)
- Calico: 35 x 20cm (14 x 8in)
- Blue kid: 3 x 8cm (1¼ x 3¼in)
- Grey kid: 5 x 8cm (2 x 3¼in)
- Bonding fabric such as
  Bondaweb: 10 x 20cm (4 x 8in)

THREADS

- Dark green rough purl:
  1m (39in)
- Grass green rough purl:
  1m (39in)
- Invisible thread
- Lime green rough purl:
  1m (39in)
- Dark grey 3-ply twist: 3m (119in)
- Brown 3-ply twist: 1m (39in)
- Dark brown 371 thread
- DMC stranded cotton: 312

TECHNIQUES

- Couched threads
  (see pages 36–38)
- Kid (see page 47)
- Fuzzy effect (see page 32)
- Appliqué (see page 22)

TEMPLATE

See page 178

ORDER OF WORK

1 Apply the brown silk to the bottom of the cream silk using the bonding fabric to secure it.

2 Transfer the design onto the joined silk using your desired method, being careful with the positioning on the two fabrics. Frame up the fabric with the calico backing.

3 Using invisible thread throughout, apply the blue and the grey kid to form the planter. Use as few stitches as possible and make them as small as you can. Around the grey kid add a line of six strands of 312, couched down with one strand at each corner.

4 Outline the feet and the top of the plinth in brown 3-ply twist couched down with invisible thread, then add a base line of 3-ply twist.

5 Fill in the feet with continuous dark brown 371 thread couched down invisible thread. To complete the plinth, twist two thicknesses of brown twist together and couch it in the gap.

6 Couch down a row of dark brown 371 with invisible thread over the join in the two fabrics.

7 Couch individual rows of dark grey 3-ply twist to form the branches and the trunk (refer to the diagram, right), using individual lengths for each one. Starting on the right-hand side, work tightly packed rows from the tip of the branch through the tree. Add rows starting along the branches to build the depth of the branches and the trunk.

8 Plunge all the ends and carefully tie back behind the embroidery.

9 To make the stone, cut a circle from the grey silk dupion measuring 3.5cm (1½in) in diameter. Run gathering stitch around the circle with the invisible thread, on the right side of the fabric and close to the edge, and pull the threads up gently to tighten slightly; this forms a natural inside edge. This is the rear of the fabric. Stitch the grey fabric in place with the invisible thread, making sure you catch the fabric in a haphazard way to form a jagged edge. The fabric will now be bulging inside the shape. Using tiny stitches, catch the fabric down, again in a haphazard formation, to give definition to the stone. Add as many stitches as you are happy with to give the overall impression.

10 Add the foliage using dark green, grass green and lime green purls in fuzzy effect. With the three colours, build the leaves adding shading and depth.

11 To finish, add a small amount of the dark green purl in fuzzy effect in the pot around the stone.

Leaves, seeds and berries

This section provides a close up of leaves, seeds and berries to give ideas of ways in which to work on a larger design, forming more intricate and detailed images. Each of the designs found here can bring wonderful highlights to your work, adding a touch of detail, colour and texture.

For this project, see pages 114–115.

Leaves Sampler

Designed and worked by Jan.

SAMPLER KEY

1. Turnover no. 1
2. Palmate (ivy leaves)
3. Turnover no. 2
4. Hastate no. 1
5. Incised
6. Hastate no. 2
7. Spiky
8. Plain
9. Bipinnate no. 1
10. Bipinnate no. 2
11. Grass no. 1
12. Grass no. 2
13. Grass no. 3

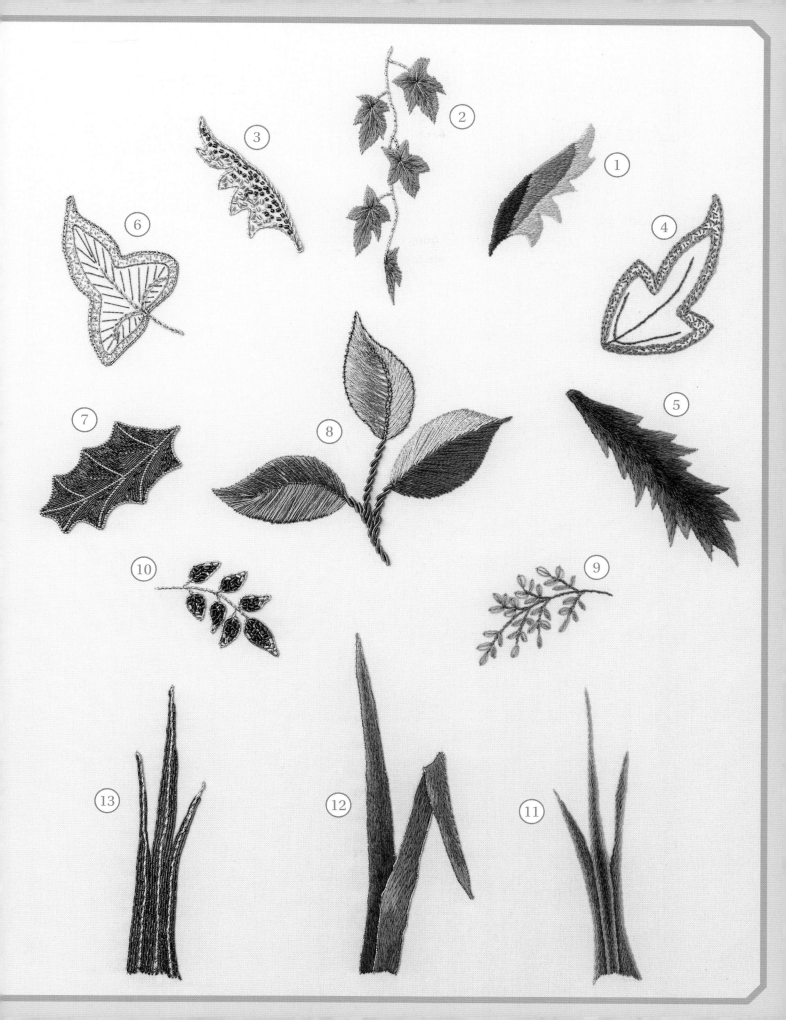

FABRIC

- Ivory silk: 40 x 40cm (16 x 16in)
- Fine calico: 40 x 40cm (16 x 16in)

THREADS & TECHNIQUES

- See each individual leaf description

TEMPLATES

See page 179

ORDER OF WORK

1 Transfer the design onto a piece of ivory silk using your chosen method.

2 Frame up, backed with fine calico.

3 These are not definitive designs, just ideas of how to work leaves. Start at the top right and work across to the left, completing each row so as not to damage any completed embroidery. (If you are left-handed, you will need to work from left to right.) Work the stranded cotton areas first, wherever possible.

1. TURNOVER NO. 1

THREADS

- DMC stranded cotton
  (use one strand throughout):
  520, 522, 524

1 Outline the complete leaf in split stitch using 524.

2 Embroider using the block shading method (see page 62). Working all the stitches horizontally Use 520 at the base, 522 in the middle and 524 at the points.

2. PALMATE (IVY LEAVES)

THREADS

- DMC stranded cotton
  (use one strand throughout):
  3364, 3363, 3362
- Gold heavy metal no. 30
- Gold check thread no. 7

1 Couch check thread no. 7 with gold heavy metal no. 30 along the stems. Use a continuous length, plunging and coming back up through the fabric where necessary and leaving 2.5cm (1in) tails at the start and the finish to plunge and sew back behind the embroidery.

2 Split stitch around each outer edge of the ivy leaves using 3364.

3 Using long-and-short stitch natural shading, shade each ivy leaf in all three colours of the stranded cotton: work from the points of the leaves, starting with the lighter shades through to the darkest at the centre.

4 Using gold heavy metal no. 30, add a straight stitch for each vein in the leaves.

3. TURNOVER NO. 2

THREADS

- Grecian twist
- Gold heavy metal no. 30
- Gold smooth passing no. 5
- Dark and light green rough purl

1 Outline the upper vein in Grecian twist, couched with heavy metal thread.

2 Outline the spiky edge with smooth passing no. 5, couched with gold heavy metal thread no. 30 and leaving 2.5cm (1in) tails at the start and end to plunge and oversew to the back of the leaf afterwards.

3 Fill the leaf with small, randomly placed chips in dark green near the back vein, getting lighter towards the spikes.

4. HASTATE NO. 1

THREADS

- DMC stranded cotton (use one strand throughout): 830, 831, 832

1 Using 832, outline the leaf with chain stitch, starting at the base of each segment and working to the points.

2 Complete a second line of chain stitches parallel inside the leaf, leaving around a 2mm (1⁄16in) gap between the lines. Fill this gap with small straight stitches in random directions using 831.

3 Stem stitch the veins using one strand of 830.

5. INCISED

THREADS

- DMC stranded cotton (use one strand throughout): 319, 699, 700, 701, 703

1 Split stitch around the leaf outline using 703.

2 Using all the shades of green, stitch the leaf with long-and-short stitch natural shading, working the lightest colour along the edges and the darkest at the centre.

6. HASTATE NO. 2

THREADS

- Gold check thread no. 7
- Gold Ophir
- Burnished gold 371
- Gold heavy metal no. 30
- DMC stranded cotton: 830

1 Outline the leaf with both check thread no. 7 and the burnished gold 371 thread laid together and couched with gold heavy metal no. 30, leaving tails and the start and end to plunge.

2 Complete a second line of couched burnished gold parallel to the outside line, leaving a 2mm (1⁄16in) gap. Fill the gap with small random straight stitches in gold Ophir.

3 Chain stitch the veins with Ophir. Add long straight stitches worked in one strand of 830 to give definition to the centre of the leaf.

7. SPIKY

THREADS

- Very fine gold pearl purl
- Gold heavy metal no. 30
- Cedar Green 371 thread
- Invisible thread

1 Outline the leaf in very fine pearl purl couched in gold heavy metal no.30.

2 Stitch the veins in very fine pearl purl couched in gold heavy metal no. 30.

3 Embroider each section in cedar green 371 using continuous couching and invisible thread.

3 Plunge all the tails and oversew to the back.

8. PLAIN

THREADS

Central leaf:
- Gold Elizabethan twist
- DMC stranded cotton: 469

Right leaf:
- Gold Ophir
- DMC stranded cotton: 469

Left leaf:
- Gold heavy metal no. 30
- DMC stranded cotton: 469

Stem:
- Green rough purl

1 For the centre leaf, use the diagonal method to complete the whole petal in Elizabethan twist (see page 46), tied down with one strand of 469.

2 Work the right leaf in two-needle leaf stitch (see page 77): use two strands of 469 for the bottom section, and gold Ophir for the top section.

3 For the left leaf, use one strand of 469 and a length of gold heavy metal no. 30 in the needle at the same time to complete the leaf in stacked fly stitch (see page 78).

4 Use green rough purl cut into 3mm (⅛in) lengths to stem stitch the stem.

9. BIPINNATE NO. 1

THREADS

- DMC stranded cotton: 987, 988, 989

1 Stem stitch the stems using one strand of 987.

2 Form each leaflet with a detached chain (five per stem), using one strand of 989 and filling with a straight stitch in 988.

10. BIPINNATE NO. 2

THREADS

- Gold Ophir
- Gold heavy metal no. 30
- Gold smooth passing no. 6
- Pale, Mid and Dark Green rough purl

1 Stem stitch the stem and veins in gold Ophir.

2 Outline the leaflets with gold no. 6 passing couched in gold heavy metal no. 30. Use one continuous length, plunging and coming up in the fabric where required.

3 Fill each leaflet with small shaded chips in dark, medium and pale green rough purl stitched down with gold heavy metal no. 30.

11. GRASS NO. 1

THREADS

- DMC stranded cotton:
  699, 700, 701, 703, 704

1 Work in rows of stem stitch, using each colour to form the shading and give depth. Work the centre blade first and then the two background blades. Use one strand throughout and pack the rows tightly together; use the lightest on the edge of the grass blade and the darkest in the centre. Colours can be changed in a row of stem stitch to give a more natural effect. Consider the light direction when working the outer two leaves.

12. GRASS NO. 2

THREADS

- DMC stranded cotton: 699, 700, 701, 703, 704
- Gold-green passing no. 4
- Invisible thread

1 Work the grass blades in long-and-short stitch natural shading. Start with the blade of grass at the back, then the base of the front blade, finishing with the turnover point. Split stitch around each section as you come to it.

2 Outline in gold-green passing no. 4 couched down with invisible thread, remembering to leave 2.5cm (1in) tails at the start and finish to plunge and sew back behind the embroidery.

13. GRASS NO. 3

THREADS

- Fine rococco gold
- Gold heavy metal no. 30
- Mid- and dark green smooth passing no. 6
- Invisible thread

1 Couch a line of fine rococco along the centre of each blade, leaving 2.5cm (1in) tails top and bottom; plunge these ends and tie back now.

2 Stitching the front blade first, outline with mid-green passing couched down in invisible thread; fill with rows of the mid-green passing packed closely together. Work each row separately.

3 For the two blades behind, outline the edge away from the central blade with mid-green passing and the edge next to the front blade with dark green passing. Fill with couched mid- and dark green, working each line separately.

4 Plunge and tie back all the ends.

One Leaf, Many Ways

Hazel created ivy-leaf designs and worked them in goldwork. Over the years these were worked in many ways by her students. Jan took inspiration from all of these to design and embroider this sampler.

FABRIC

- Green silk dupion: 15 x 35cm (6 x 14in)
- Calico: 15 x 35cm (6 x 14in)

MATERIALS

- DMC stranded cotton: 831, 832, 833, 834
- Gold heavy metal no. 30
- Gold kid: 5 x 5cm (2 x 2in)
- Elizabethan twist
- Gold Ophir
- Very fine gold pearl purl: 40cm (16in)
- Gold bright check purl no. 8: 50cm (20in)
- Gold smooth purl no. 8: 75cm (29½in)
- Gold smooth passing no. 6: 20cm (8in)
- Old gold smooth purl no. 8: 50cm (20in)
- Pale gold smooth purl no. 8: 50cm (20in)
- Gold check thread no. 7: 15cm (6in)

TECHNIQUES

- Two-needle leaf stitch (see page 77)
- Split stitch (see page 60)
- Long-and-short stitch natural shading (see page 64)
- Chain stitch (see page 77)
- Satin stitch padding (see page 20)
- Satin stitch (see page 75)
- Stem stitch (see page 74)
- Couched threads (see pages 36–38)
- Elizabethan twist (see page 46)
- Kid (see page 47)
- Fuzzy effect (see page 32)
- Stacked fly stitch (see page 75)
- Shaded chippings (see page 32)
- Graded cutwork (see page 33)

TEMPLATE

See page 178

ORDER OF WORK

Transfer the design onto the green silk using your chosen method (do not add the numbers, they are just for reference) then frame up with the calico backing. Work the stems first to allow smooth lines to be created; these are worked in stem stitch with gold Ophir. If a leaf features couching, plunge and oversew the tails to the back before working the next leaf.

LEAF 1

Using one strand of 832, work the leaf in two-needle leaf stitch.

LEAF 2

Split stitch around the edge in one strand of 832. Work the leaf shading using single strands of 831, 832, 833 and 834 using long-and-short stitch natural shading (see the direction diagram, right).

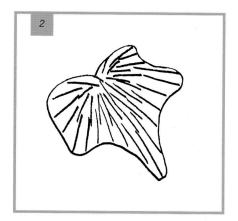

LEAF 3

Outline the leaf and add veins in one strand of 832 using chain stitch. Fill the leaf with tiny irregular straight stitches worked in both 833 and 834, again using one strand.

LEAF 4

Outline the leaf with split stitch using one strand of 833. Add a layer of satin stitch padding, again using one strand. Satin stitch the leaf with two strands of 833 at a diagonal angle (see the direction diagram, right). Outline the leaf with gold Ophir couched down with a gold heavy metal no. 30.

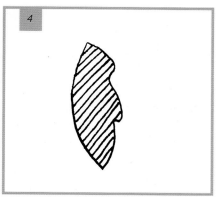

LEAF 5

Using Elizabethan twist traditional method, couch down the Elizabethan twist with one strand of 831.

LEAF 6

Cut the leaf out in gold kid and stitch into position with gold heavy metal no. 30. Outline with gold check thread no. 7 couched with gold heavy metal no. 30.

LEAF 7

Outline the leaf with three strands of 834 couched with one strand of the same thread. Fill the leaf in with fuzzy effect using old gold smooth purl.

LEAF 8

Thread the needle with one strand of 834 and one length of gold heavy metal no. 30 and work the leaf in stacked fly stitch.

LEAF 9

Outline the leaf and add the veins in very fine pearl purl secured with gold heavy metal no. 30. Fill the leaf in with shaded chips, using old gold, gold and light gold smooth purl no. 8, shading to form a dark centre with lighter edges.

LEAF 11

Outline the leaf in very fine gold pearl purl stitched down with gold heavy metal no. 30. Fill the leaf with gold cutwork, alternating bright check no. 8 and smooth purl no. 8 (see the direction diagram above).

LEAF 10

Outline the leaf and add veins in gold smooth passing no. 6 couched in gold heavy metal no. 30. Add a few chips along the veins, lightly spaced in gold smooth purl no. 8.

Berries and Seeds Sampler

Each of these ideas can be used in conjunction with a larger piece of embroidery, as an embellishment or simply as part of the overall design. Remember these are just ideas – have fun with your own creations. Designed by Hazel; worked by Jan.

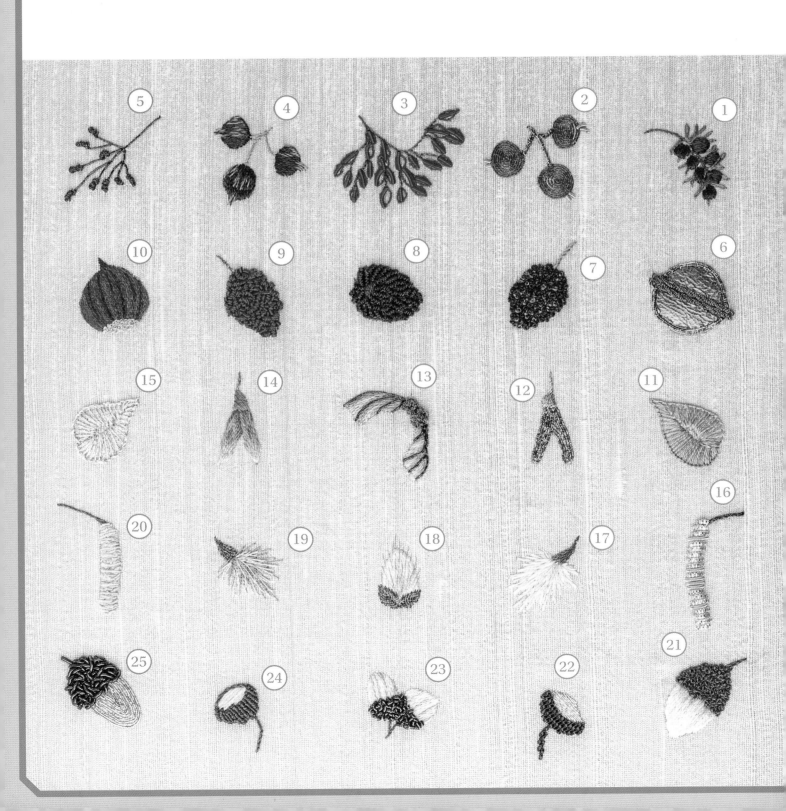

SAMPLER KEY

1. Juniper berries
2. Redcurrants
3. Wayfaring tree berries
4. Blackcurrants
5. Rowan berries
6. Walnut
7. Blackberry
8. Mulberry
9. Raspberry
10. Chestnut
11. Elm seed no. 1
12. Seedpod no. 1
13. Sycamore seeds
14. Seedpod no. 2
15. Elm seed no. 2
16. Catkin no. 1
17. Catkin no. 2
18. Catkin no. 3
19. Catkin no. 4
20. Catkin no. 5
21. Acorn no. 1
22. Acorn no. 2
23. Acorn no. 3
24. Acorn no. 4
25. Acorn no. 5

ORDER OF WORK

1 Transfer the design onto the silk using your desired method and frame up with the calico backing.

2 Work the seeds and berries from the top row down and right to left, so as not to damage any work completed. (If you are left-handed, work from left to right.) Wherever possible, complete the work in stranded cotton first.

FABRIC

- Beige silk: 40 x 40cm (16 x 16in)
- Calico: 40 x 40cm (16 x 16in)

THREADS & TECHNIQUES

- See each individual berry or seed description

TEMPLATE

See page 180

1. JUNIPER BERRIES (SEE OPPOSITE)

THREADS

- DMC stranded cotton (one strand unless stated otherwise): 433, 469, 3799

1 Stem stitch the stalk in 433. Add irregular single chain stitches along the length of the stalk in 469 to form the spiky leaves.

2 Outline each berry in split stitch and sew one layer of satin stitch padding using 3799. Using two strands of 3799, vertically satin stitch each berry from its top to its base.

2. REDCURRANTS (SEE OPPOSITE)

THREADS

- Red 371 thread
- Beige rough purl
- Green 3-ply twist
- Invisible thread

1 Work each currant in a continuous spiral of red 371 thread held down with invisible thread: start at the edge of the currant and work in.

2 Attach two small chips of beige rough purl to form the top of each currant.

3 Couch green 3-ply twist to form the stems, remembering to leave 2.5cm (1in) at the start and finish for plunging.

3. WAYFARING TREE BERRIES

THREADS

- DMC stranded cotton
  (use one strand throughout):
  3362, 321
- Red rough purl
- Invisible thread

1 Stem stitch the stalk in 3362.

2 For each of the berries, work a detached chain stitch in 321 and add an extra small stitch either side to tie down the chain in an oval.

3 Fill each berry with a chip of red rough purl stitched with invisible thread. Cut them slightly longer than the chain stitch to form a curve when stitched; this adds depth to the berry.

4. BLACKCURRANTS

THREADS

- DMC stranded cotton:
  470, 3799, 317

1 Stem stitch the stalk using one strand of 470.

2 Split stitch around the currants using one strand of 3799.

3 Long-and-short stitch tapestry shade the currants using one strand of 3799, then highlight with 317.

5. ROWAN BERRIES

THREADS

- Brown passing
- DMC Jewel Effects: E815
- Invisible thread

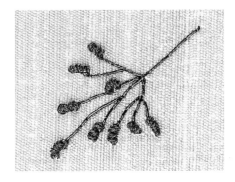

1 Stitch a row of brown passing couched with invisible thread to form the stems.

2 Using two strands of E815, add a bullion knot to form the berry at the end of each stem.

6. WALNUT

MATERIALS

- Gold kid
- Burnished gold 371 thread
- Old gold 3-ply twist
- Gold heavy metal no. 30
- Invisible thread

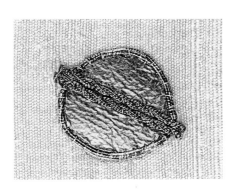

1 Cut out the whole nut shape in kid and stitch into position using gold heavy metal no. 30.

2 Stitch two rows of old gold twist along the centre of the nut, overlapping at either side. Couch with invisible thread. Plunge the ends straight away and oversew to the back.

3 Outline the top and bottom of the nut with two rows of burnished gold 371 couched down with gold heavy metal no. 30.

7. BLACKBERRY

THREADS

- DMC stranded cotton: 470, 3799, 317

1 Stem stitch the stalk using two strands of 470.

2 French knot the blackberry. For the main body of the berry use two strands of 3799. Then, around the edge and at intervals over the berry, use one strand each of 3799 and 317 in the needle at the same time to add a little light and texture.

8. MULBERRY

THREADS

- DMC stranded cotton: 315
- Dark wine check purl
- Invisible thread

1 Work individual chain stitches in one strand of 315 to form the edge of each segment: start at the base of the fruit and work to the top (see diagram, left).

2 Satin stitch the top centre.

3 Add a long chip of dark wine check purl tied down with invisible thread to fill every chain stitch; make sure these lie flat.

9. RASPBERRY

THREADS

- Green 371 thread
- Red smooth purl
- Red wire check purl
- Invisible thread

1 Using green 371 thread, stem stitch the stalk.

2 With small chips, fill the raspberry shape using red smooth purl and red wire check purl stitched with invisible thread. Add them in a haphazard way for a natural appearance.

10. CHESTNUT

THREADS

- DMC stranded cotton (use one strand throughout): 300, 400, 3782

1 Fill the top with straight stitches using 300.

1 Work rows of stem stitch tightly packed together following the shape of the chestnut; use 300 and 400, and work from the centre out.

2 Fill the base with French knots using 3782.

11. ELM SEED NO. 1

THREADS

- DMC stranded cotton:
  523, 522

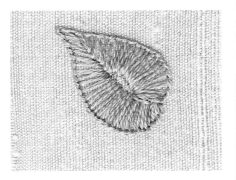

1 Using one strand each of 523 and 522 in the needle, buttonhole around the elm seed, starting at the base and working round, tapering where needed. Take the stitches to the centre to form the vein (see diagram, below).

12. SEEDPOD NO. 1

THREADS

- Burnished gold passing
- Gold heavy metal no. 30
- DMC Light Effects: E436

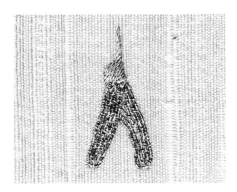

1 For the wings, couch down burnished gold passing with gold heavy metal no. 30, and in continuous couching. Start on the outside and work in. At the end, plunge all the tails and oversew to the back.

2 Stem stitch the stalk using one strand of E436.

3 Satin stitch the seed using one strand of E436.

13. SYCAMORE SEEDS

THREADS

- DMC stranded cotton:
  611, 612, 613, 371
- Green smooth purl
- Brown 371 thread
- Green 371 thread
- Invisible thread

1 Embroider the seed wings in rows of stem stitch using single strands of 611, 612 and 613, shading to form the veins.

2 Couch brown 371 thread with invisible thread to highlight the veins on the wings. Plunge then oversew the ends to the back.

3 Outline the seeds at the top with couched green 371 thread and fill with green purl fuzzy effect (see page 32).

14. SEEDPOD NO. 2

THREADS

- DMC stranded cotton
  (use one strand throughout):
  611, 612, 613

1 Split stitch the edge of the wings in 612.

2 Work long-and-short stitch natural shading in all three shades to fill the wings, starting at the tips with the lightest shade.

3 Split stitch around the seed pod cap and then satin stitch in 611.

4 Stem stitch the stalk in 611.

15. ELM SEED NO. 2

THREADS

- DMC Light Effects: E966
- DMC Light Effects: E677

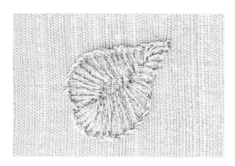

1 Using one strand of E966 and one strand of E677 in the needle at the same time, buttonhole around the elm seed, starting at the base and working around, tapering where needed. Take the stitches to the centre to form the vein (see diagram, below).

16. CATKIN NO. 1

THREADS

- Dark brown 3-ply twist
- Soft cotton padding
- Lime green wire check purl
- Lime smooth purl
- Invisible thread

1 Couch dark brown 3-ply twist with invisible thread to form the stalk. Plunge then oversew the ends to the back.

2 Add a row of soft cotton padding down the length of the catkin.

3 Lay chips of lime green wire check purl and lime smooth purl horizontally over the soft cotton padding, stitched down with invisible thread, to form the catkin.

17. CATKIN NO. 2

THREADS

- DMC stranded cotton:
  869, 822, 472, 165

1 Using one strand of 869, embroider tapered rows of stem stitch to form a stalk.

2 Complete the catkin with irregular straight stitches worked in two strands of 822, 472 and 165 in an irregular formation, building each colour separately to add depth and interest.

18. CATKIN NO. 3

THREADS

- DMC stranded cotton: 648, 644, 822
- Gold heavy metal no. 30
- Copper heavy metal no. 12

1 Use long-and-short stitch shading to fill the centre dome of the catkin using single strands of 648, 644 and 822. Keep the edges uneven for a more natural effect.

2 Add straight stitches in gold heavy metal no. 30 for highlights.

3 Work rows of stacked fly stitch in copper heavy metal no. 12 to form the base.

19. CATKIN NO. 4

THREADS

- Champagne, sunrise and lime green 371 threads
- Copper heavy metal no. 12

1 Using copper heavy metal no. 12, embroider rows of stem stitch to form the tapered stalk.

2 Complete the catkins with irregular straight stitches, worked in champagne, sunrise and lime green 371 threads.

20. CATKIN NO. 5

THREADS

- DMC stranded cotton: 869, 165, 472

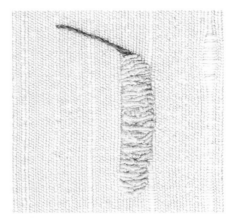

1 Stem stitch the stalk using one strand of 869.

2 Stitch rows of bullion knots worked in single strands of 165 and 472. Start at the base and work upwards.

21. ACORN NO. 1

THREADS

- DMC stranded cotton: 3865, 822, 3782, 839

1 Split stitch the edge of the nut using one strand of 3865.

2 Use long-and-short stitch tapestry shading to infill the nut using single strands of 3865, 822 and 3782.

3 Stem stitch the stalk using two strands of 839.

4 Complete the cup with French knots using two strands of 839.

22. ACORN NO. 2

THREADS

- DMC Light Effects: E168
- Dark brown wire check purl

1 Satin stitch the inside of the cup using one strand of E168.

2 Using dark brown check purl cut to 3mm (⅛in) lengths, stem stitch the stalk.

3 Use cutwork to complete the cup using dark brown check purl, cutting each chip to the required length.

23. ACORN NO. 3

THREADS

- DMC stranded cotton: 839, 3865, 822, 3782
- Dark brown smooth purl
- Medium brown smooth purl

1 Stem stitch the stalks using one strand of 839.

2 Complete the nuts, working rows of stem stitch with single strands of 3865, 822 and 3782.

3 Fill the back cup with tiny chips of dark brown purl. For the front cup, fill with tiny chips of medium brown purl.

24. ACORN NO. 4

THREADS

- DMC stranded cotton: 822, 839

1 Satin stitch the inside of the cup using one strand of 822.

2 Stem stitch the stalk and around the outside base of the cup using two strands of 839.

3 Using two strands of 839, fill in the cup with bullion knots.

25. ACORN NO. 5

THREADS

- Soft gold passing
- Invisible thread
- Dark brown purl
- Medium brown purl

1 Couch soft gold passing continuously around the nut, stitched down with invisible thread. Start from the outside and work in. Plunge then oversew the ends to the back.

2 Stem stitch the stalk in dark brown purl.

3 Complete the cup in dark and medium brown purl chips. Cut the purl into 6mm (¼in) lengths and stitch down in an irregular pattern of loops which overlap each other.

Acorns

Designed by Hazel; embroidered by Jan.

FABRIC

- Green silk dupion: 15 x 15cm (6 x 6in)
- Felt: 5 x 5cm (2 x 2in)
- Calico: 15 x 15cm (6 x 6in)

THREADS

- DMC stranded cotton: 822, 613, 612, 611, 610
- Brown passing: 40cm (16in)
- Soft cotton padding
- Brown 3-ply twist: 75cm (29½in)
- Invisible thread
- Brown wire check no. 8: 175cm (69in)

TECHNIQUES

- Felt padding (see page 20)
- Bump/soft cotton padding (see page 21)
- Long-and-short stitch natural shading (see page 64)
- Split stitch (see page 60)
- Graded cutwork (see page 33)
- Couched threads (see pages 36–38)

TEMPLATE

See page 184

ORDER OF WORK

1 Transfer the design onto the green silk using your chosen method then frame up with the calico backing.

2 Add the felt padding for the cups and nuts: add one layer of padding for all no. 2 acorns, and two layers for all no. 3 acorns (see diagram below).

3 Add soft cotton padding just in the cup areas to pad one layer for all no. 2 acorns and two layers for all no. 3 acorns.

4 Split stitch around each nut using one strand of 610.

5 Shade each nut with long-and-short stitch using one strand of cotton throughout. Use 610, 611, 612, 613 and 822, shading where appropriate.

6 For each of the stems, couch one row of brown 3-ply twist with one row of brown passing next to it using invisible thread. Work each stem individually, leaving 2.5cm (1in) at the start and end of each to plunge. Plunge all ends and oversew back behind the stems.

7 Outline each cup with brown 3-ply twist, starting and ending at the stem each time. Plunge and sew back the tails.

8 Complete the cups in cutwork using brown wire check no. 8 stitched down with invisible thread. Make sure each chip fits nicely into the 3-ply twist edge and that they lay smoothly next to each other, completely covering the fabric.

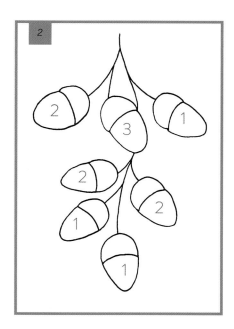

Fronds and fungi

Fronds and fungi can make beautiful embellishments in any design. Unfortunately, there is limited choice of green colours in metal threads for these. However, embroidery threads mitigate this with numerous textures and shades, lending themselves to the delicacy of the foliage and intricacy of the fungi.

A simple grouping of fronds worked in various different techniques is an elegant way to produce a sampler. Each frond is worked using a different medium and technique, each balancing to form an elegant design in its own right.

Fronds Sampler

Designed by Hazel; worked by Jan.

SAMPLER KEY

1. Frond no. 1
2. Frond no. 2
3. Frond no. 3
4. Frond no. 4
5. Frond no. 5
6. Frond no. 6
7. Frond no. 7
8. Frond no. 8
9. Frond no. 9
10. Frond no. 10
11. Frond no. 11
12. Frond no. 12

FABRIC

- Cream silk dupion: 25 x 35cm (10 x 14in)
- Calico: 25 x 35cm (10 x 14in)

THREADS & TECHNIQUES

- See each individual frond description

TEMPLATE

See page 181

ORDER OF WORK

1 Transfer the design onto the cream silk using your desired method then frame up with the calico backing.

2 Work the fronds from the top row down and right to left (left to right, if you are left-handed), so as not to damage any work completed. Wherever possible, complete the work in stranded cotton first.

1. FROND NO. 1

THREADS

- Green and gold milliary
- Gold heavy metal no. 30

1 Couch a row of green and gold milliary (see page 41) around the shape, stitched with gold heavy metal no. 30.

2. FROND NO. 2

THREADS

- DMC stranded cotton (use one strand throughout): 470, 471, 472
- Gold check thread no. 7
- Gold heavy metal no. 30

1 Split stitch around the leaves using 472.

2 Using long-and-short stitch natural shading, infill the leaves using 472, 471 and 470, shading where appropriate.

3 Couch gold check thread no. 7 along the stalk with gold heavy metal. Use one continuous length and be careful when plunging to oversew along the line of the stalk, so there are no visible ridges on the right side of the embroidery.

3. FROND NO. 3

THREADS

- DMC stranded cotton (use one strand throughout): 3345, 832

1 Stem stitch the stalk using 3345.

2 Embroider the leaves in two-needle leaf stitch (see page 77) using 3345 on one side and 832 on the other.

4. FROND NO. 4

THREADS

- DMC stranded cotton: 304, 699

1 Stem stitch the stalk using one strand of 699.

2 Embroider each leaf with small chain stitch in one strand of 699, being careful not to pull them tight so the leaves are a nice shape.

3 At the end of the stem and between each pair of leaves add three berries. These are French knots worked in two strands of 304: one French knot equals one berry.

5. FROND NO. 5

THREADS

- DMC Light Effects (use one strand throughout): E699, E815

1 Stem stitch the stalk using E699.

2 Embroider the leaves with E699 using stacked fly stitch (see page 75).

3 Add the berries with French knots using E815: stitch one cluster at the end of the stem and two clusters between the leaves.

6. FROND NO. 6

THREADS

- Green 371 thread

1 Using green 371 thread, stem stitch the stalk.

2 Where the small markings are indicated along the stalk, add two straight stitches in green 371, one either side of the stalk. Vary the length to add interest and to make them more realistic.

7. FROND NO. 7

MATERIALS

- DMC stranded cotton: 936

1 Using two strands of 936, split stitch the stalk.

2 Where the small markings are indicated along the stalk, embroider four straight stitches using two strands of 936 – two either side of the stem, one short above one long.

8. FROND NO. 8

THREADS

- Green passing
- Invisible thread

1 Use green passing couched down with invisible thread in one continuous length (see the diagram below for the direction, starting at the dot).

9. FROND NO. 9

THREADS

- DMC stranded cotton: 3818

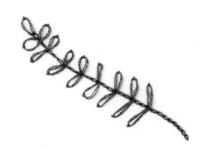

1 Chain stitch using one strand of 3818 to form the stalk.

2 At each small mark on the stem work a loose chain stitch using two strands of 3818, one either side of the stem.

10. FROND NO. 10

THREADS

- DMC stranded cotton (use one strand throughout): 3346, 3347, 3348

1 Stem stitch the stalk using 3346.

2 Split stitch around each leaf in 3348.

3 Use long-and-short stitch natural shading to fill the leaves using 3348, 3347 and 3346, shading where appropriate.

11. FROND NO. 11

THREADS

- Green opal 371 thread
- Gold Ophir
- Invisible thread

1 Couch down green opal 371 thread with invisible thread for the stem. Plunge then oversew the tails to the back.

2 Satin stitch each leaf using gold Ophir.

12. FROND NO. 12

1 Using one strand of 700, satin stitch the frond with diagonal stitches (see diagram, right).

2 Couch down green passing with invisible thread around the fern, touching but not over the satin stitch.

Fungi Sampler

A colourful addition to any piece of work. Designed by Hazel; worked by Jan.

SAMPLER KEY

1. Fungus no. 1
2. Fungus no. 2
3. Fungus no. 3
4. Fungus no. 4
5. Fungus no. 5
6. Fungus no. 6
7. Fungus no. 7
8. Fungus no. 8
9. Fungus no. 9
10. Fungus no. 10

FABRIC

- Beige silk dupion: 25 x 35cm (10 x 14in)
- Calico: 25 x 35cm (10 x 14in)

THREADS & TECHNIQUES

- See each individual fungus description

TEMPLATES

See page 182

1. FUNGUS NO. 1

MATERIALS

- Felt: 5 x 5cm (2 x 2in)
- DMC stranded cotton: 640, 642, 644, 822, 3782

ORDER OF WORK

1 Transfer the design onto the silk using your desired method and then frame up with the calico backing.

2 Begin by applying the cap of the top-left mushroom (fungus no. 3; the template is on page 182). I have used a shot black and gold silk to add texture. This is not an easy fabric to apply as it frays quickly.

3 Work the fungi from the top row down and right to left (left to right, if you are left-handed), so as not to damage any work completed. Wherever possible, complete the work in stranded cotton first.

1 Add one layer of felt to the top of the mushroom cap (see template, page 182).

2 Work the underside of the cap in bullion knots packed closely together, spiralling out from the centre using one strand of 640.

3 Stem stitch the stalk in two strands of 822 and 3782, shading where desired. The stalk is worked in two sections – do not stitch over the central ridge, called a ring. Fill the ring with French knots embroidered in two strands of 822.

4 Split stitch around the outer edge of the top of the mushroom in two strands of 644. Use long-and-short stitch natural shading to fill the cap using two strands of 640, 644 and 642, starting with the darkest at the top.

2. FUNGUS NO. 2

THREADS

- DMC stranded cotton (use two strands throughout): 822, 3782
- Nut crunch passing
- Copper heavy metal no. 30

1 Split stitch the outline of the stalk using 3782.

2 Use long-and-short stitch tapestry shading to fill the stalk with 3782 and 822.

3 Use nut crunch passing couched with copper heavy metal no. 30 to continuously couch the cap. Start at the top outside edge and work in rows until the cap is full, turning at the base of the cap each time. Plunge then oversew the ends to the back.

3. FUNGUS NO. 3

THREADS

- Silver Ophir
- Silver check thread no. 7
- Silver heavy metal no. 30
- Silver rococco

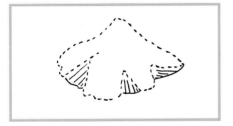

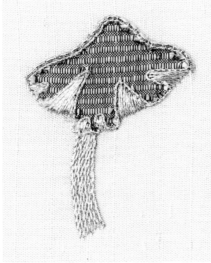

1 Stem stitch the stalk in silver Ophir.

2 Outline the fabric applied at the beginning with silver check thread no. 7 couched down with silver heavy metal. Take the check thread up and around the indents to make the shape (see diagram, left). Plunge then oversew the tails to the back.

3 Using silver Ophir, satin stitch all the shaded areas in the cap: cover those outside the check thread but over the applied fabric.

4 Add a row of fine silver rococco attached with silver heavy metal along the top of the cap.

4. FUNGUS NO. 4

THREADS

- Red 371 thread
- Invisible thread
- Silver wire check purl no. 8
- Red smooth check purl no. 8
- Silver Ophir
- Gold heavy metal no. 12

1 Satin stitch the underside of the cap (the gills) in silver Ophir.

2 Stem stitch the stalk in rows using gold heavy metal no. 12.

3 Couch a row of red 371 thread around the outside of the cap, stitched down with invisible thread. Plunge then oversew the ends to the back.

4 Add chips of silver wire check purl no. 8 for the spots.

5 Complete the cap by filling with chips of red smooth purl no. 8.

5. FUNGUS NO. 5

THREADS

- DMC stranded cotton: 321, 822, 3782

1 Use buttonhole stitch to fill the underside of the mushroom cap (the gills) using one strand of 822. Place the loop of the buttonhole around the edge of the cap.

2 Stem stitch the stalk using one strand of 822. Start at the right and work left, packing the stitches close together. Add a row on each edge in one strand of 3782 as shading.

3 Embroider the white spots in the cap using French knots worked in two strands of 822.

4 Complete the cap with French knots worked in one strand of 321.

6. FUNGUS NO. 6

MATERIALS

- Purple kid
- Silver passing no. 13
- Silver heavy metal no. 30
- White opal and gold 3-ply twist
- Gold 371 thread
- Gold heavy metal no. 30
- Silver milliary

1 Apply purple kid for the cap, using the overall template given on page 182.

2 Attach a couched white opal and gold 3-ply twist down the centre of the stem. Then add two lines of gold 371 thread couched either side of the twist with gold heavy metal no. 30.

3 Outline the top of the cap with two rows of silver passing no. 13, couched down with silver heavy metal no. 30.

4 Couch one row of silver passing and one of silver milliary (see page 41) along the bottom of the cap.

7. FUNGUS NO. 7

THREADS

- DMC stranded cotton: 3041, 3042, 3743, 3865

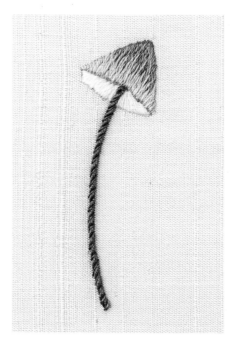

1 Split stitch the outer edge of the underside of the cap using one strand of 3865. Then satin stitch the area in the same thread.

2 Couch a handmade cord made out of six strands of 3041 for the stem.

3 Split stitch around the cap using one strand of 3743. Infill the cap with long-and-short stitch tapestry shading using single strands of 3041, 3042 and 3743, starting at the top with the darkest shade.

8. FUNGUS NO. 8

THREADS

- DMC stranded cotton
  (use one strand throughout):
  728, 727, 3078, 746

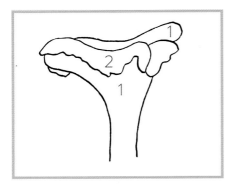

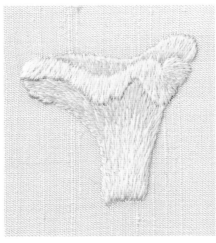

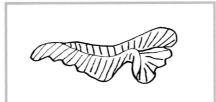

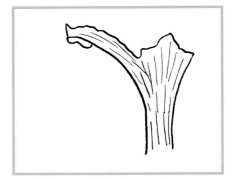

1 Use a combination of 728, 727, 3078 and 746 as you work the following areas. Start with the no. 1 areas (see diagram, below left): split stitch the outlines, then embroider with long-and-short stitch natural shading.

2 Split stitch the outside edge of area no. 2 then use long-and-short stitch natural shading to fill this area, referring to the stitch direction diagrams below.

9. FUNGUS NO. 9

THREADS

- Silver heavy metal no. 12
- DMC stranded cotton
  (use one strand throughout):
  304, 666, 321, 822
- Soft gold passing
- Gold heavy metal no. 30
- Silver smooth purl no. 8

1 Work the gills in silver heavy metal no. 12: work along the base in buttonhole stitch and satin stitch over the upper section. (Do not worry about leaving gaps.)

2 Split stitch around the cap in 304. Using 666, 321 and 304, fill the cap with long-and-short stitch tapestry shading, leaving empty holes for the spots.

3 For the stalk, work from the outside in on both sides. Couch down two rows of soft gold passing with gold heavy metal no. 30. Add one row of chain stitch worked using 827. Add four rows of passing – these should split into pairs as they reach the bottom of the stalk. Between these split pairs, work a small row of chain stitch, then on each side of this row fill the spaces with two small rows of passing. Finish with a central row of chain stitch. Plunge then oversew the ends to the back.

4 Complete the cap by working the spots with silver smooth purl chips cut very small and stitched down with silver heavy metal no. 12.

10. FUNGUS NO. 10

THREADS

- White opal 3-ply twist
- Gold soft passing
- Invisible thread
- Dark grey rough purl
- Light grey rough purl
- Silver rough purl

1 To fill the stalk, couch rows of white opal 3-ply twist and soft gold passing, stitched down with invisible thread. Plunge then oversew the ends to the back.

2 Complete the head in fuzzy effect (see page 32), building the shape using dark and light grey purls and silver purl to form a shaded effect. Couch down with invisible thread.

Butterflies, bats and dragonflies

This book would not be complete without a section of flying creatures. Hazel loved all animals and was particularly drawn to those that many of us are less interested in. What follows is just a small selection of Hazel's favourites.

For this project, see page 142–143.

Three Butterflies

Butterflies meant a great deal to Hazel and she loved watching them in her beautiful garden. The delicacy and colour found on many butterflies makes them the perfect subject for a piece of embroidery.

Here, one butterfly is worked in silk shading, one in goldwork and one using both techniques – to show the versatility and also the difference each medium provides. These butterflies are inspired by the monarch butterfly, taken from a sketch found in Hazel's drawings and embroidered by Jan. The template can be found on page 183.

FABRIC

- Green-gold shot silk dupion: 35 x 35cm (14 x 14in)
- Calico: 35 x 35cm (14 x 14in) and 10 x 10cm (4 x 4in)
- Orange felt: 10 x 10cm (4 x 4in)

MATERIALS

Silkwork butterfly (bottom left):

- DMC stranded cotton: 310, 919, 920, 921, 922
- Two silver beads

Goldwork butterfly (top right):

- Copper superfine pearl purl: 30cm (12in)
- Copper heavy metal no. 30
- Copper very fine rococco: 75cm (29½in)
- Black opal 371 thread: 75cm (29½in)
- Copper 371 thread: 50cm (20in)
- Copper rough purl: 25cm (10in)
- Light copper rough purl: 25cm (10in)

- Ginger smooth purl: 25cm (10in)
- Black rough purl: 50cm (20in)
- Three silver beads
- Copper heavy metal no. 12
- Invisible thread

Mixed butterfly (centre):

- DMC stranded cotton: 310
- Copper heavy metal no. 30
- Copper superfine pearl purl: 25cm (10in)
- Copper heavy metal no. 12
- Copper rough purl no. 8: 20cm (8in)
- Copper bright check no. 8: 15cm (6in)
- Copper 371 thread: 75cm (29½in)
- Copper very fine rococco: 160cm (63in)
- Copper rough purl: 30cm (12in)
- Light copper rough purl: 30cm (12in)
- Ginger smooth purl: 30cm (12in)
- Two silver beads
- Fine wire: 40cm (16in)

TECHNIQUES

Silkwork butterfly (bottom left):

- Long-and-short natural shading (see page 64)
- Split stitch (see page 60)
- Stem stitch (see page 74)
- French knots (see page 76)
- Bullion knots (see page 76)

Goldwork butterfly (top right):

- Couched threads (see pages 36–38)
- Shaded chippings (see page 32)

Mixed butterfly (centre):

- Long-and-short stitch natural shading (see page 64)
- Split stitch (see page 60)
- Couched threads (see pages 36–38)
- Satin stitch (see page 75)
- Graded cutwork (see page 33)
- Shaded chippings (see page 32)
- Buttonhole stitch (see page 74)

ORDER OF WORK

Transfer the main design onto the green-gold shot silk using your desired method; do not transfer any three-dimensional elements or the antennae. Frame up with the larger piece of calico backing. Transfer the two three-dimensional wings of the mixed butterfly onto the smaller piece of calico to work separately.

SILKWORK BUTTERFLY (BOTTOM LEFT)

1 Use one strand of cotton throughout. Split stitch around the back wing using 310. Work the wing in long-and-short stitch natural shading, starting at the edge in 310 and keeping this around the outer edge. Complete the wing using just 920 and 919, as this is all in shadow. Make sure the blending between the black and the copper is uneven.

2 Split stitch around the edge of the top section of the front wing in 310. Work the wing in long-and-short stitch natural shading with 310 around the edge and then 922, 921, 920 and 919 within, shading where appropriate.

3 Complete the bottom of the front wing in the same way.

4 With one strand of 310, stem stitch the antennae.

5 Fill the head with French knots using 310.

6 Fill the body with bullion knots using 310.

7 Add two silver beads on the top of the two upper wings in the black areas.

GOLDWORK BUTTERFLY (TOP RIGHT)

1 Couch copper superfine pearl purl around the outside of each wing, stitched down with copper heavy metal no. 30.

2 Couch down copper very fine rococco with copper heavy metal no. 30 around each of the detail shapes in the wings, plunging at the end of one segment and bringing up at the start of the next using one continuous thread; leave 2.5cm (1in) tails at the start and end. Plunge the tails and sew back behind the embroidery.

3 On the rear wing, embroider the outer area in continuous couching using black opal 371 thread stitched down with invisible thread. Complete the rear wing by filling the two colourful shapes in continuous couching using copper 371 thread stitched down with copper heavy metal no. 30. Plunge all ends and stitch back.

4 Fill the coloured sections on the wings in the foreground in tiny shaded chips of copper, light copper and ginger rough purl.

5 Fill the edge section of the foreground wings with tiny black purl chips and two silver beads for the spots. Add a third bead to the rear wing.

6 Work the antennae in stem stitch using copper heavy metal no. 12.

7 Fill the head with French knots made with copper heavy metal no. 12. Fill the body with bullion knots made with copper heavy metal no. 12.

MIXED BUTTERFLY (CENTRE)

1 On the main design, pad the body with two thicknesses of felt (refer to page 183 for the templates): start with the three small separate pieces for the head, body and tail, and then the one overall piece is placed over the top to cover all three and fill the whole shape.

2 Using one strand of 310, split stitch around the two lower wings. Fill the area of the outside of the wing in long-and-short stitch natural shading using 310.

3 In the quarter-circle area where each lower wing meets the body, work buttonhole stitch, wheeling around the shape, and add a straight stitch of copper heavy metal no. 12 in between each buttonhole stitch.

4 Couch the outline of the head and then the body in copper superfine pearl purl stitched down with copper heavy metal no. 30. Then add the antennae with copper superfine pearl purl, again stitched down with copper heavy metal no. 30.

5 Satin stitch the head in copper heavy metal no. 12.

6 Fill the body and tail in cutwork: complete the body in copper bright check purl no. 8 and the tail in copper no. 8 rough purl.

7 Outline the bottom two wings with couched very fine rococco and 371 thread, with the rococco along the outer edge and stitched down with copper heavy metal no. 30.

8 Outline the colourful shapes in each wing with very fine rococco, stitched down with copper heavy metal no. 30. Plunge all the tails.

9 Fill these shapes with tiny shaded chips of copper, light copper and ginger purl.

THREE-DIMENSIONAL WINGS

1 On the separate piece of calico, place the fine wire just inside the outline of the two upper wings and couch down with 310.

2 Buttonhole around the edge of the wings and over the wire using 310.

3 Complete the upper wings in the same way as the bottom wings on the mixed butterfly (see the steps above), adding a silver bead around the top section of each wing before you chip.

4 Carefully cut the wings out.

5 Attach the wings to the body of the mixed butterfly. Position the wings and then plunge the wire, rococco and 371 and oversew behind the body.

6 Stitch tiny stitches in copper heavy metal no. 30 to hold the wings in place.

3D Gold and Silkwork Butterfly

Designed and worked by Hazel.

FABRIC

- Pale blue silk dupion:
  20 x 20cm (8 x 8in)
- Calico: 20 x 20cm (8 x 8in)
- Ultrasuede: 15 x 15cm
  (6 x 6in)

MATERIALS

- DMC stranded cotton:
  939, 798, 747, 598, 208
- Gold broad plate: 20cm (8in)
- Fine gold pearl purl: 20cm (8in)
- Gold wire check purl no. 7:
  60cm (24cm)
- Two gold beads
- Fine wire: 1m (39in)
- String: 40cm (15¾in)
- Soft cotton: 20cm (8in)
- Gold heavy metal no. 30
- PVA glue

TECHNIQUES

- Buttonhole stitch (see page 74)
- Split stitch (see page 60)
- Bump/soft cotton padding
  (see page 21)
- Long-and-short stitch with
  natural definition (see page 65)
- Plate (see pages 48–49)
- Graded cutwork (see page 33)
- Couched threads
  (see pages 36–38)
- String (see page 21)

TEMPLATE

See page 185

ORDER OF WORK

1 Transfer the design onto the ultra-suede using your chosen method, but don't mark on the antennae.

2 Couch a double row of fine wire around the edge of the wings. Begin in the body section, attaching it in the centre, and sewing a line up the centre of the body. Then work around the wings, placing the wire a fraction in from the edge. When one side has been completed, cross over the body and couch around the second side. Finish the wire in the body and secure with several stitches. I used one strand of 939 for securing the couching.

3 Pad the body with a length of string, running it down the centre from top to bottom. Put a smaller length of string either side and soften the padding with several stitches in soft cotton/bump over the top of the string.

4 Work buttonhole stitch over the wire on the wings with one strand of 939 – start next to the body and pack the stitches closely together, altering the length of the stitches to add extra stability. Make sure the buttonhole stitches are at right angles to the design line.

5 To work the top wings, use one strand of stranded cotton throughout. Begin by embroidering lines of split stitch in 939 to form the veins. Complete the wings in long-and-short stitch natural shading. Start with 939, bringing the needle up in the wing and taking it down just inside the beaded edge of the buttonhole. Try to keep the stitches running parallel to the split stitch veins. Then work a row of long-and-short stitch in 208, 747, 598 and finally 798 next to the body. For all these rows make sure the needle is brought up through the preceding stitches, piercing the thread. This will give a smoother appearance.

6 To work the bottom wings, work in exactly the same way but do not use the 747. Outline each wing with gold wire check purl no. 7 stitched down with gold heavy metal no. 30.

7 To complete the bottom half of the body work broad plate over the string (see diagram, below right). Starting at the bottom, form a small hook on the end of the plate. Using waxed thread, attach the hook beside the string. Take a small stitch in the fabric (very close to the string) to secure the hook. Work the plate over the string lapping it left and right, always taking a stitch over the plate at the side of the string to secure.

8 Outline the whole body with fine gold pearl purl couched with gold heavy metal no. 30. Then, to complete the top half of the body, work in cutwork using gold wire check purl. Be careful to cut the lengths accurately to allow them to sit neatly over the string. Add two gold beads at the top for the eyes.

9 Once all the embroidery is complete, coat the back of the butterfly with PVA glue and allow it to dry thoroughly. Cut off the bulk of the excess ultrasuede, leaving a seam allowance of 5mm (¼in). Now it should be easier to cut close to the goldwork – trim as close to the embroidery as possible.

10 Frame up the background silk dupion with the calico backing, and on this add two pearl purl antennae. Stitch a 5mm (¼in) length of the pearl purl down at the head area with gold heavy metal no. 30, leaving the rest of the pearl purl free.

11 Place the butterfly in position over the antennae. Plunge the couched threads into the background fabric and oversew behind the body. Next, carefully sew the body of the butterfly into place with small stitches, making sure the stitches are along the edge of the body where it joins with the wings only, so the stitches are completely hidden.

12 Gently bend the wings and antennae into the desired positions.

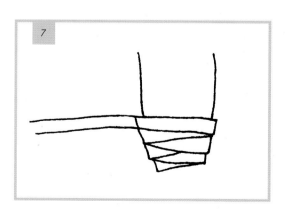

Three Bats

I found this bat design with Hazel's drawings and a photocopy of the finished piece in metallic threads. I felt it was perfect to adapt to show the difference in goldwork and silk shading threads and the design's simplicity, which can be so effective.

FABRIC

- Dark grey silk dupion: 25 x 30cm (10 x 12in)
- Calico: 25 x 30cm (10 x 12in)

MATERIALS

Silkwork bat (top left):
- DMC stranded cotton: 3024, 535

Goldwork bat (bottom right):
- Silver Ophir
- Silver heavy metal no. 30

Mixed bat (centre):
- DMC stranded cotton: 3024, 535
- Silver heavy metal no. 30
- Silver Ophir

TECHNIQUES

- Straight stitch (see page 75)
- Couched threads (see pages 36–38)
- Split stitch (see page 60)

TEMPLATE

See page 184

ORDER OF WORK

Transfer the design onto the fabric using your chosen method, then frame up with the calico backing.

SILKWORK BAT (TOP LEFT)

1 Outline the wings in couching: use three strands of 3024 as the laid thread stitched down with one strand of 3024. Start at the base of the body, leaving a tail to plunge. Work all the way around the wing to the body and then plunge and come up on the other side of the body to couch around the other wing. Plunge and sew back the tails.

2 Couch the veins in the wings with one strand of 3024 stitched with one strand of 3024.

3 With irregular straight stitches and one strand of 3024, fill in the body. Start from the bottom and work up, keeping the outline irregular so that it looks natural. Do not worry if there are a few small gaps. This stitch is much like a very open long-and-short stitch, coming up in the fabric and down in the previous row.

4 Split stitch around the head using one strand of 3024 then work irregular straight stitches over the split stitch.

5 Lastly, add small straight stitches for the definition of the eyes, nose and ears in 535.

GOLDWORK BAT (BOTTOM RIGHT)

1 Outline the wings with silver Ophir couched with silver heavy metal no. 30. Work each wing separately. Add the veins in the same way.

2 Embroider the body in silver Ophir, starting at the tail and working along the body in irregular straight stitches, keeping the edge uneven.

3 Split stitch around the head and then embroider in irregular straight stitches over the split stitch in the same way as the body.

MIXED BAT (CENTRE)

1 Work the wings in the same way as for the goldwork bat (see above), using silver Ophir and silver heavy metal no. 30.

2 Work the bat itself in the same way as for the silkwork bat (see above).

Bat

A bat is an unusual inspiration for embroidery, but it was an obvious choice for me as it reminds me so much of Hazel. She had a love of bats – bats and Hazel were synonymous with each other, and this is my tribute to her. This design was adapted from a tattoo I found on the internet. It can be worked in a small frame, encompasses a variety of techniques to give interest and provide a taste of several different mediums.

FABRIC

- Silver grey silk dupion: 25 x 25cm (10 x 10in)
- Calico: 25 x 25cm (10 x 10in)
- Black kid: 10 x 10cm (4 x 4in)
- Grey felt: 5 x 5cm (2 x 2in)

THREADS

- Silver Ophir
- DMC stranded cotton: 310, 413, 640, 642
- Silver heavy metal thread, no. 30
- Silver metallic purl: 20cm (8in)
- Silver rough purl: 20cm (8in)
- Silver 371 thread: 2m (79in)
- Very fine silver rococo: 1m (39in)

TECHNIQUES

- Split stitch (see page 60)
- Long-and-short stitch (see pages 64–65)
- Satin stitch (see page 75)
- Two-needle leaf stitch (see page 77)
- Purl chippings (see page 31)
- Kid (see page 47)
- Bullion knots (see page 76)
- Couched threads (see pages 36–38)
- Chain stitch (see page 77)

TEMPLATE

See page 185

ORDER OF WORK

1 Transfer the design onto the fabric using your desired method and then frame up with the calico backing.

2 Trace and cut out the kid wings and then apply them to the fabric.

3 Mark the veins on the wings with a chalk pencil.

4 For the outside edges of both the wings, couch down two lengths of silver 371 at the same time with silver heavy metal thread no. 30. Then add the veins to the wings using two lengths of silver 371 thread for the right-hand wing and just one length of 371 on the left-hand wing. Leave the tails of the 371 to take down and fasten off behind the embroidery at the start and end of each length. Plunge these when all the couching is complete.

5 Attach a layer of felt to completely cover the head. This is used here to balance the height of the head with the wings so that it does not appear to sink behind the wings but appears slightly forward. Make sure you mark on the eyes and nose.

6 Plan the long-and-short stitches for the bat head, first preparing a sketch for the shading and order of work (see **6a**, below right) then another for the stitch direction (see **6b**, below right).

7 Split stitch around the edge of the bat's head using 640. Work the long-and-short stitch with natural definition over the face, except for the features, using single strands of 310, 413, 640 and 642.

8 Work the nose in 310 using long-and-short stitch with natural definition, then work satin stitch either side to fill in any spaces that are left.

9 For the whiskers, add five or six very long stitches either side of the nose in 310.

10 Split stitch around the edge of the eyes using one strand of 310 and then satin stitch over the top with two strands of 310.

11 Split stitch around the outside edge of the leg. Use long-and-short stitch natural shading and 310 to infill the leg.

12 To work the main branch, couch three rows of silver very fine rococco thread stitched with silver heavy metal no. 30 (leave tails of 2.5cm or 1in at the start and finish). Plunge the ends and sew back on the reverse of the embroidery.

13 Work each leaf in two-needle leaf stitch using silver Ophir. Complete each leaf with a stem worked in stem stitch to join it to the main branch.

14 Work each raspberry in the same way: first work the main berry, using tiny chippings of silver metallic purl chips around the outer edges and silver rough purl chips in the centre, stitched with silver heavy metal no. 30. Do not outline the berry, as you want to keep this knobbly natural edge. Then embroider the sepals at the berry head in silver Ophir. Each sepal is a chain stitch with a long chip of silver metallic purl stitched down the centre.

15 Add the claws over the main branch using 310: make two bullion knots starting in the fabric and ending on the main branch.

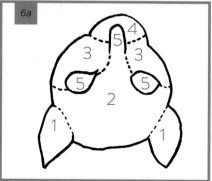

6a

6b

Bats

I found a sketch of this design in Hazel's notes and, as it is so
beautiful, I chose to work it for this section.

FABRIC

- Silver-grey silk dupion:
  30 x 25cm (12 x 10in)
- Calico: 25 x 25cm (10 x 10in)
- Soft black kid: 10 x 10cm
  (4 x 4in)

THREADS

- Black Gütermann thread
- DMC stranded cotton: 310
- 3-ply silver twist: 1m (39in)
- Silver heavy metal no. 30
- Silver baby Grecian twist:
  40cm (16in)
- Silver Ophir

TECHNIQUES

- Kid (see page 47)
- Twists (see page 39)
- Stem stitch (see page 74)
- Satin stitch (see page 75)

TEMPLATE

See page 185

ORDER OF WORK

1 Transfer the design onto the silk dupion using your desired method and then frame up the fabric with the calico backing.

2 Carefully cut out each bat from the black soft kid and stitch into position with black Gütermann thread.

3 Outline each bat with six strands of 310, couched down with one strand of 310.

4 Next add the swirls. Using silver heavy metal no. 30 for the stitching and leaving 2.5cm (1in) tails at the start and end, couch 3-ply silver twist on all the swirls with long dashes (see the diagram below). Couch silver baby Grecian twist along the solid line swirls. Add stem stitched silver Ophir along the swirls with short dashes. Plunge and sew back all the tails.

5 Satin stitch the large swirl with silver Ophir.

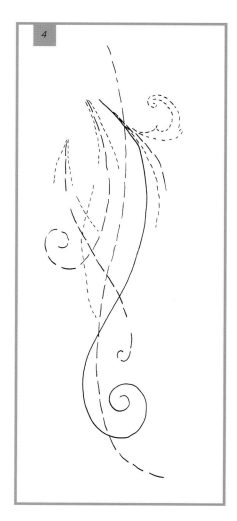

Three Dragonflies

Hazel loved dragonflies and embroidered them throughout her career.
This sampler was based on an image I found when going through some of
her work and felt it could be used to depict the three styles of embroidery
highlighted in this book.

FABRIC

- Ivory silk dupion: 25 x 30cm (10 x 12in)
- Calico: 25 x 30cm (10 x 12in)
- Grey organza: 10 x 20cm (4 x 8in)
- Iron-on adhesive such as Bondaweb: 10 x 10cm (4 x 4in)
- Felt: 2 x 2cm (¾ x ¾in)

MATERIALS

- Tiny amount of black purl or six tiny beads

Silkwork dragonfly (bottom left):
- Grey heavy metal no. 30
- DMC Light Effects: E317
- DMC stranded cotton: 747, 3761, 996, 995, 414

Goldwork dragonfly (top right):
- Grey heavy metal no. 30
- Silver heavy metal no. 30
- DMC Light Effects: E317
- Silver Ophir
- Electric twist purl: 5cm (2in)
- Electric shimmer purl: 5cm (2in)
- Stonewash glimmer purl: 5cm (2in)
- Supa blue wire check purl: 5cm (2in)

Mixed dragonfly (centre):
- Grey heavy metal no. 30
- Silver heavy metal no. 30
- DMC Light Effects: E317
- Silver Ophir
- DMC stranded cotton: 996, 995
- Silver passing no. 6: 25cm (10in)
- Electric twist purl: 5cm (2in)
- Electric shimmer purl: 5cm (2in)

- Stonewash glimmer purl: 5cm (2in)
- Supa blue wire check purl: 5cm (2in)

TECHNIQUES

- Long-and-short stitch natural shading (see page 64)
- Split stitch (see page 60)
- Appliqué (see page 22)
- Couched threads (see pages 36–38)
- Purl chippings (see page 31)
- Buttonhole stitch (see page 74)
- Satin stitch (see page 75)
- Chain stitch (see page 77)
- Felt padding (see page 20)

TEMPLATES

See page 186

ORDER OF WORK

1 Transfer the design onto the silk dupion using your chosen method – only transfer the bodies; do not draw the wings on (all the wings will be drawn on the organza and then either couched down or attached three-dimensionally).

2 Prepare the wings: fuse iron-on adhesive to one end of the organza then fold the other half over and iron together, forming a firm two-layered piece of fabric for the wings. Draw the wings onto the organza.

SILKWORK DRAGONFLY (BOTTOM LEFT)

1 Cut out the wings (refer to page 186). Using grey heavy metal no. 30, stitch the wings in position on the body – use small stitches 2mm (⅟₁₆in) apart. Outline the four individual wings with two strands of E317 couched down with grey heavy metal no. 30, leaving 2.5cm (1in) of thread at the start and end to plunge. Work in a continuous thread, starting with the two background wings and then the two wings in front, taking the thread down behind the body when crossing over. Plunge the start and end tails and oversew in place to finish off. With one strand of the E317, stitch long stitches in each of the wings for definition. Then add two straight stitches on the head for the antennae and two at the end for the tip of the tail.

2 Use one strand throughout and work each section of the tail in the same way, first split stitching around the edge and then using long-and-short stitch to fill the section. Split stitch around the bottom tail section in 747. Then, using 747 and 3761, long-and-short stitch shade the first section. For the next two sections, add split stitch in 3761 and long-and-short stitch in 3761 and 996. For the last two sections, add split stitch in 996 and long-and-short stitch in 996 and 995.

3 Split stitch around the body in 995. Then satin stitch a layer of padding horizontally in 995 to almost fill the body. Apply long-and-short stitch shading in 996 and 995 over the top of the satin padding to complete the body.

4 Using 414, split stitch around the head, then add long-and-short stitch to the area in the same thread.

5 Add two very tiny black chips either side of the head for the eyes.

GOLDWORK DRAGONFLY (TOP RIGHT)

1 Cut the two pairs of wings out of the organza. Place the background pair into position and, using grey heavy metal no. 30, stitch into place around the edge using small stitches approximately 2mm (1/16in) apart. Outline the wings using two strands of E317, couched down with grey heavy metal no. 30; leave 2.5cm (1in) tails at the start and finish and work in a continuous thread. Plunge the ends and oversew to finish.

2 With one strand of E317, add three straight stitches to each wing for definition. Then add two straight stitches for antennae on the head and two on the end of the tail.

3 For the front pair of wings do not cut out, but couch around the edge of the wings with two strands of E317 with grey heavy metal no. 30, leaving 2.5cm (1in) tails at the start and finish. Add three long straight stitches for decoration using one strand of E317.

4 Cut out the wings as close to the couching as possible and sew in place on the body of the dragonfly. Plunge the tails through the main fabric and oversew behind the embroidery.

5 Satin stitch the head using silver Ophir.

6 For the body and tail, use single chain stitches to outline the shape of each segment using silver Ophir. Starting from the top of the body, fill the chain stitches with the following long purl chips, stitched down with silver heavy metal no. 30:
- Body: three electric twist purl chips.
- Top tail section: one electric twist purl chip and one electric shimmer purl chip either side.
- Second tail section: three electric shimmer purl chips.
- Third tail section: one stonewash glimmer purl chip with one electric shimmer purl chip either side.
- Fourth tail section: one supa blue wire check chip with one stonewash glimmer purl chip either side.
- Bottom tail section: three supa blue wire check chips.

7 Add two very tiny black chips either side of the head for the eyes.

MIXED DRAGONFLY (CENTRE)

1 All four wings will be three-dimensional. Do not cut the wings out yet. Using grey heavy metal no. 30, couch two strands of E317 around the edges of both pairs of wings, leaving 2.5cm (1in) tails at the start and end for plunging. Add three straight stitches in one strand of E317 for wing definition. Cut the wings out carefully and position them on the body. Apply the wings to the body by plunging the tails and oversewing them behind the body.

2 With one strand of E317, stitch two straight stitches for the antennae and then two at the base for the tail. Satin stitch the head in silver Ophir.

3 Trim the square of felt to the shape of the body, cut slightly smaller around. Couch it over the body to add a little height and then work over this in long-and-short stitch natural shading using 996 and 995 (there is no need to add a split stitch outline, as we will outline in the next step).

4 Outline the body and then each section of the tail in silver passing no. 6, couched down with silver heavy metal no. 30. Use one continuous length, and leave 2.5cm (1in) tails at the start and finish to plunge and oversew behind the embroidery.

5 Starting at the top end of the tail, fill each segment with tiny chips:
- Top tail section: electric twist purl chips.
- Tail sections 2 and 3: electric shimmer purl chips.
- Tail section 4: stonewash glimmer purl chips.
- Bottom tail section: supa blue wire check purl chips.

6 Add a very small black chip either side of the head for the eyes.

Large Dragonfly

Designed by Hazel; worked by Jan.

FABRIC

- Dark blue silk dupion: 25 x 25cm (10 x 10in)
- Calico: 25 x 25cm (10 x 10in)
- Green and gold shot organza: 20 x 6cm (8 x 2½in)
- Fusible web, such as Bondaweb: 20 x 6cm (8 x 2½in)

MATERIALS

- Gold heavy metal no. 30
- DMC stranded cotton: 734, 733, 732, 731, 730
- Green-gold milliary: 75cm (29½in)
- Smooth passing no. 4: 2m (80in) (cut into four 50cm/20in lengths)
- Gold Ophir
- Pale leaf wire purl: 25cm (10cm)
- Two green glass 8mm beads

TECHNIQUES

- Appliqué (see page 22)
- Milliary (see page 41)
- Couched threads (see pages 36–38)
- Long-and-short stitch tapestry shading (see page 63)
- Split stitch (see page 60)
- Satin stitch (see page 75)
- Fuzzy effect (see page 32)

TEMPLATES

See page 187

ORDER OF WORK

1 Transfer the design for the body and head onto the silk dupion fabric using your chosen method; do not draw the wings on.

2 To prepare the wings, lay a piece of fusible web that is bigger than the wing template over the reversed side of the design, so that the paper is uppermost. Trace on the design with a pencil. Iron the piece of fusible web onto the organza. Allow to cool down then carefully cut out the design. Peel off the paper backing. Turn the appliqué over and place in position on the silk background fabric, sticky side down. If you wish, place a covering cloth over the wings, then gently iron in place.

3 Frame up the silk dupion background with the appliqué with the calico backing fabric.

4 Couch the green-gold milliary around the edge of the wings: start with the top wings then couch the lower wings. Work each wing individually, leaving 2.5cm (1in) tails at the start and finish for plunging.

5 Add definition to the wings with veins using a single row of gold smooth passing couched with evenly spaced stitches in gold heavy metal no. 30. Use one continuous length for each individual wing, leaving 2.5cm (1in) tails to plunge at the start and finish of each length of passing.

6 Plunge all ends through and oversew in place.

7 Embroider the tail. Starting at the base and using one strand of cotton throughout, split stitch around the bottom tail section in 734. Fill in the segment working long-and-short tapestry shading – light to dark – using 734, 733 and 732. Complete the next section up in exactly the same way. For the next section, split stitch in 733 and embroider in long-and-short stitch tapestry shading using 733, 732 and 731, again from light to dark. Repeat for the next section. For the final section nearest the body, split stitch around the edge in 732 and embroider in long-and-short stitch tapestry shading using 372, 371 and 370.

8 Outline each tail segment with couched gold passing, using one continuous thread stitched down with gold heavy metal no. 30. Be very careful not to shred it as you take it through the fabric.

9 Add two couched lines from the bottom edge of the tail for the tail ends.

10 Outline the head, eyes, antennae and body with couched gold passing, stitched down with gold heavy metal thread no. 30.

11 Fill the head with satin stitch in gold Ophir. Attach two green glass beads for the eyes.

12 Complete the body with fuzzy effect using pale leaf wire purl couched in gold heavy metal no. 30. Manipulate the thread to cover the whole area.

SEASONAL PROJECTS

This section contains four complete projects. The first is the embroidery on the front cover, which represents springtime. This is followed by designs inspired by summer, autumn and winter.

Clematis Early Semi-double Dr. Ruppel

This is one of Hazel's very last designs. She had only drawn it and not yet decided how it was going to be worked. I have chosen the techniques hoping the final piece is as she would have wished and a testament to the beauty of the combination of metal threadwork and silk shading.

ORDER OF WORK

1 Transfer the design onto the larger piece of silk using your chosen method then frame up with the calico backing. Mark on the stems as single lines only and do not mark on any petals that are going to be three-dimensional (they are shown with dashed lines, below). Mark these petals onto the smaller piece of silk, leaving 2cm (¾in) in between each; mark which is which for ease when positioning, once worked.

2 Begin by working the silk shaded areas (see the diagram above for the order of work: work sections 1, 2, 3, 4 and 5). For each element, split stitch around the shape first then complete in long-and-short stitch natural shading, using one strand throughout (refer to the diagrams below for stitch direction guides). Make sure the split stitches are worked in the same colour as the one which will cover it. The leaves are embroidered in a combination of 904, 905, 906 and 907. The petals are worked in a combination of 915, 917, 3607, 3608 and 3609. The buds are a combination of 915, 917, 3608, 907 and 906.

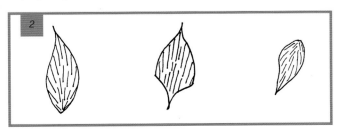

Stitch direction guides for leaves (left), petals (centre) and buds (right).

FABRIC

- Cream silk dupion: 40 x 40cm (16 x 16in) and 28 x 28cm (11 x 11in)
- Calico: 40 x 40cm (16 x 16in) and 28 x 28cm (11 x 11in)

THREADS

Flowers:
- DMC stranded cotton: 915, 917, 3607, 3608, 3609
- Silver check thread no. 7: 5.5m (217in)
- Silver heavy metal no. 30
- Silver rough purl: 1.5m (59in)
- Viola rough purl: 1.5m (59in)
- Fuchsia smooth purl: 1.5m (59in)

Leaves:
- DMC stranded cotton: 904, 905, 906, 907
- Gold check thread no. 7: 3.5m (138in)
- Gold heavy metal no. 30

Stem:
- DMC stranded cotton: 904
- Green 3-ply twist: 2m (79in)
- Gold check thread no. 7: 50cm (20in)
- Gold heavy metal no. 30
- Silver-plated wire, 0.2mm diameter: 3m (118in)
- PVA glue

TECHNIQUES

- Split stitch (see page 60)
- Long-and-short stitch natural shading (see page 64)
- Twists (see pages 39)
- Couched threads (see pages 36–38)
- Shaded chippings (see page 32)
- Fuzzy effect (see page 32)
- Buttonhole stitch (see page 74)

TEMPLATES

See pages 188–189

3 Cut a length of silver check thread no. 7 to 75cm (29½in). Leaving a 2.5cm (1in) tail to plunge, start by couching the check thread around the outer edge of a flower centre with silver heavy metal. Take the check thread down through the fabric when complete and bring it back up at one edge of a front petal; repeat until all front petals have been outlined (be very careful when you do this not to damage any of the embroidery), then take the thread through the fabric to the larger back petals and repeat, couching around them until they have all been outlined. Repeat for each flower. Plunge the start and finish tails and oversew behind the embroidery.

4 Using green 3-ply twist couched with one strand of waxed 904, embroider the stems. Leave 2.5cm (1in) tails at the beginning and end of each stem (do not use continuous lengths for this – work each section of the stem independently); the 3-ply twist will finish at the base of the leaves or behind a petal. Couch gold check thread no. 7 with gold heavy metal on the top side of each stem as a highlight; continue this couching up into the leaf to form the central vein. Again, leave 2.5cm (1in) tails at the start and end, working each stem independently. Plunge all the tails and fasten off behind the embroidery.

5 Couch gold check thread around the edge of each leaf with gold heavy metal no. 30, starting and ending each side of the stem and leaving 2.5cm (1in) tails. Complete all the leaves in the same way. Plunge all ends and finish behind the embroidery.

6 Couch down silver check thread with silver heavy metal no. 30 around the edge of the buds: begin and end at each side of the stem, leaving 2.5cm (1in) tails. Complete all the buds and finish by plunging the tails and sewing behind the embroidery.

7 For each foreground petal on the main design, embroider inside the check thread outlines with shaded chips of smooth fuchsia purl, viola purl and silver rough purl. For shading, start with a silver purl chip edge and work inwards, then add the fuchsia purl chips and lastly, in the centre of the petals, complete with the viola purl chips, mixing the three colours so there are no hard lines.

8 Now turn your attention to the separate piece of fabric where the three-dimensional petals have been drawn. Work each petal in the same way. Couch two pieces of fine wire together just inside the edge of the outline, using silver heavy metal thread and placing the stitches approximately 2mm (⅛in) apart. Cross the wires over at the lower edge and couch together. Leave long 5cm (2in) ends (see diagram, above right). Now work buttonhole stitch in silver heavy metal no. 30 around the edge of each petal, over the wire. Start at the bottom between the overhanging wires. Make the buttonhole stitches irregular in length to help stabilize the fabric when the petal is cut out and keep them very close together to form a good firm edge. Fasten off and start new threads anywhere within the petal.

9 Couch silver check thread no. 7 with silver heavy metal no. 30 along the two sides of the petal. Leave 2.5cm (1in) tails at the start and end for plunging, and make sure your couching stitches are inside the loops of buttonhole stitch and that the check thread lays over the top of the wire. Embroider each petal with shaded chips in the same way as the flat petals on the main design. Do not complete the bottom edges, as these will be finished when they are attached to the main piece of work. Once the embroidery is complete, coat the back of each petal with PVA glue and allow to dry thoroughly.

10 Cut off the bulk of the excess fabric so the petals are easier to handle, then cut the remaining fabric away when you are ready to work each individual petal. Trim as close as possible to the buttonhole stitching using very sharp, fine pointed scissors. Position a petal in place (refer to the diagram opposite or on page 189 for positioning) and plunge the check thread and wires. Finish off by oversewing behind the embroidery. Oversew the base of the petal using tiny stitches in silver heavy metal no. 30 where it joins the centre of the flower. Cover the join with purl chips to finish off the petal. Repeat for the remaining petals.

11 With gold smooth purl use fuzzy effect to fill the centre of each flower, couched down with gold heavy metal thread no. 30.

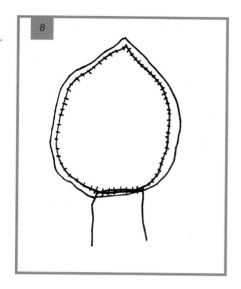

Summer Wildlife Garden

Hazel loved the beautiful textures and colours of a summer scene, and a wildlife garden encapsulates everything she enjoyed: the delicate shapes, the myriad colours and the little beasts that are all present. This design is truly a celebration of Hazel. This piece was designed by Hazel and worked by Elaine Brum, one of Hazel's students.

FABRIC

- Dark blue silk dupion: 40 x 40cm (16 x 16in)
- Calico: 40 x 40cm (16 x 16in)

THREADS

Sunflowers:

- Gold passing no. 4: 22cm (8½in)
- Gold rough purl: 14cm (5½in)
- Brown rough purl: 23cm (9in)
- Dark green 3-ply twist: 15cm (6in)
- Dark green 371 thread: 50cm (20in)
- DMC stranded cotton: 701, 909
- Gold heavy metal no. 30
- Invisible thread

Cornflowers:

- DMC Jewel Effect: E3843
- DMC stranded cotton: 895

Hedgehog:

- DMC stranded cotton: 839, 840, 841, 842
- Soft gold 371 thread: 2m (79in)
- Burnt copper 371 thread: 2m (79in)
- Small black bead

Hollyhocks:

- Light green 3-ply twist: 82cm (32¼in)
- Pink rough purl: 50cm (20in)
- Silver-lined gold beads
- Light green 371 thread: 50cm (20in)
- DMC stranded cotton 701, 909
- Invisible thread

Petunias:

- DMC stranded cotton: 909
- Dark pink smooth purl: 50cm (20in)
- Gold smooth purl no. 8: 5cm (2in)

Dragonfly:

- Silver Ophir

Butterfly:

- Gold Ophir
- Gold heavy metal no. 30

Daisies:

- Silver Ophir
- Light green 371 thread: 50cm (20in)
- DMC stranded cotton: 973, 725
- Invisible thread

Buddleia:

- DMC stranded cotton: 909, 327, 3740

Snail:

- Gold Ophir
- Gold 3-ply twist: 20cm (8in)
- Gold heavy metal no. 30

Grass:

- Light green 371 thread: 2m (79in)

TECHNIQUES

- Couched threads (see pages 36–38)
- Long-and-short stitch natural shading (see page 64)
- Fuzzy effect (see page 32)
- Detached chain (see page 77)
- French knots (see page 76)
- Stem stitch (see page 74)
- Straight stitch (see page 75)
- Purl loops (see page 35)
- Purl chippings (see page 31)
- Satin stitch (see page 75)
- Bullion knots (see page 76)
- Split stitch (see page 60)
- Straight stitch (see page 75)

TEMPLATE

See page 190

ORDER OF WORK

1 Transfer the design onto the fabric using your chosen method. Make sure you only mark on the lines that will be covered, and do not mark the numbers – these are for reference when completing the stitching below. Some general rules to follow when transferring the design:

- For stems use a single line only.
- For the petunias and daisies, only mark the centre of the flower, not the petals.
- For the hollyhocks and cornflowers, do not mark the flower at all – only the stems and leaves.
- For the buddleia, only mark the stems, not the flowers or the leaves.
- For the dragonfly, do not mark the wings, only the body.
- Do not mark on the grass at the base in the foreground (refer to the template at this stage – it can look confusing, but it will become apparent when embroidering).

2 Frame up using your desired method. A slate frame would be best for this kind of work. Remember to add the calico backing – it's very important for a piece of work this size.

3 For any couching, ensure that you leave 2.5cm (1in) tails at the start and finish, then plunge and oversew these to the back of the embroidery after working the couched area..

1. BUDDLEIA

Using one strand of 909, stem stitch the stems. Add satin stitch for the leaves using three to five stitches – place these to your preference to balance the overall appearance of the buddleia. At the end of each stem, embroider a flower: work a mixture of bullion knots and French knots using single strands of 327 and 3740.

2. SUNFLOWERS

For them stem, couch down a dark green 3-ply twist with invisible thread. Infill the leaves in long-and-short stitch natural shading using single strands of 701 and 909. Outline the leaves in couched dark green 371 thread. For the flower, outline each petal with couched gold passing no. 4 using gold heavy metal thread no. 30 for the stitching, and use one continuous thread. From the gold rough purl cut long gold chips measuring the full length of each petal and add them to the centre of each with gold heavy metal no. 30. Complete the flower centre with fuzzy effect using brown rough purl, tied down with gold heavy metal no. 30.

3. CORNFLOWERS

Stem stitch each stem using one strand of 895, then add long straight stitches for the leaves using the same thread. Add as many leaves as you like. Using E3843, embroider the flowers and the buds with straight stitches of varying lengths and directions, radiating from the flower centres.

4. DAISIES

Couch light green 371 for stems using invisible thread. To work the flower petals, embroider single chain stitches around the centre of each flower – so that they touch each other – using silver Ophir. Fill the centre of the flowers with French knots, worked in single strands of 973 and 725.

5. HOLLYHOCKS (STEMS)

Couch down light green 3-ply twist using invisible thread for the stem. Embroider the leaves with long-and-short stitch natural shading using single strands of 701 and 909 and form the central vein with stem stitch. Outline each leaf with couched green 371 thread secured with invisible thread (the flowers are completed later).

6. PETUNIAS (STEMS)

Stem stitch the stems using one strand of 909 (the flower is completed later).

7. DRAGONFLY

The dragonfly is embroidered in silver Ophir. Add four wings – two either side of the body and close to the head – using individual (detached) chain stitches, one for each wing. Satin stitch the head. Complete the body with a bullion knot.

8. BUTTERFLIES

The butterflies are embroidered in gold Ophir and each butterfly is worked in the same way. Couch gold Ophir with gold heavy metal no. 30 around each wing. Add two or three straight stitches in each wing to add definition and interest. Embroider two small straight stitches at the top of the head with a French knot at the end of each one for the antennae. Work a small bullion knot for the head and then add a larger bullion knot below for the body.

9. SNAIL (ON THE SUNFLOWER STEM)

Couch a small, compact spiral of gold 3-ply twist for the shell, stitched down with gold heavy metal no. 30. Satin stitch the head and tail in gold Ophir.

10. HEDGEHOG

Split stitch around the face of the hedgehog using one strand of 841. Using 839, 840, 841 and 842, use long-and-short stitch natural shading to complete the face. Add a small black bead for the eye. Cover the body with irregular straight stitches in 371 threads: soft gold and burnt copper.

11. GRASS

Add grass along the base of the design using light green 371. Embroider straight stitches of varying lengths and directions. Add as much or as little grass as you like.

5. HOLLYHOCKS (FLOWERS)

Cut lengths of pink rough purl; for the top flowers, cut the lengths approximately 5mm (¼in) long, gradually getting longer until the lengths are 2.5cm (1in) long for the bottom flowers. With each length make fuzzy effect balls for the flowerheads. Stitch these down with invisible thread and add a gold bead to some of the flowerheads. Position each flower along the stem in an irregular way to look as natural as possible.

6. PETUNIAS (FLOWERS)

Cut lengths of dark pink smooth purl approximately 5mm (¼in) in length to form loops around the centre of the flower. Add five loops to make each flower. Add a small chip of gold smooth purl for the centre.

Autumn

Hazel designed this piece a few years ago and it was worked in many different ways by her students, mainly just in goldwork. This is my interpretation of the piece using Hazel's ideas from throughout this book.

FABRIC

- Dark brown silk dupion: 20 x 30cm (8 x 12in)
- Calico: 20 x 30cm (8 x 12in)

THREADS

Catkins:
- Champagne, sunrise and lime green, 371 threads: 50cm (20in) of each

Laurel leaf:
- DMC stranded cotton: 470
- Copper heavy metal no. 30

Stalks:
- Copper heavy metal no. 12

Horse chestnut leaf:
- DMC stranded cotton: 300, 301, 471, 472

Maple leaf:
- Dark brown, dark copper and light copper rough purl no. 8: 50cm (20in) of each

- Dark brown 3-ply twist: 50cm (20in)
- Invisible thread

Rowan berries:
- DMC stranded cotton: 321
- Invisible thread
- Old gold rough purl: 5cm (2in)

Oak leaf:
- Nut crunch 371: 3m (119in)
- Dark brown 3-ply twist: 50cm (20in)
- Invisible thread

Ash leaves:
- DMC stranded cotton: 780, 781, 782, 918

Acorns:
- Dark brown passing: 20cm (8in)
- Dark brown check purl: 30cm (12in)
- Invisible thread
- DMC stranded cotton: 822, 610, 611, 612, 613

TECHNIQUES

- Straight stitch (see page 75)
- Stacked fly stitch (see page 75)
- Stem stitch (see page 74)
- Long-and-short stitch (see pages 61–65)
- Split stitch (see page 60)
- Couched threads (see pages 36–38)
- Shaded chippings (see page 32)
- Satin stitch (see page 75)
- Purl chippings (see page 31)

TEMPLATE

See page 191

ORDER OF WORK

Transfer the design to the fabric and frame up with the calico backing (do not transfer the numbers – these relate to the instructions below). Throughout, remember to leave 2.5cm (1in) tails at the start and end of any couching to plunge and stitch back behind the embroidery.

1. ASH LEAVES

Stem stitch the stalk in copper heavy metal no. 12. Split stitch around each leaflet using one strand of 782, then infill each leaflet with long-and-short stitch natural shading using single strands of 782, 781, 780 and 918. Start from the points of the leaf and work towards the stem.

2. HORSE CHESTNUT

Stem stitch the stalk in copper heavy metal no. 12. Split stitch around each leaflet using one strand of 300, then shade the leaves with long-and-short stitch natural shading using single strands of 300, 301, 471 and 472. Keep the brown towards the edges and the green in the centre; start at the points and work towards the centre (refer to the stitch direction diagram, right).

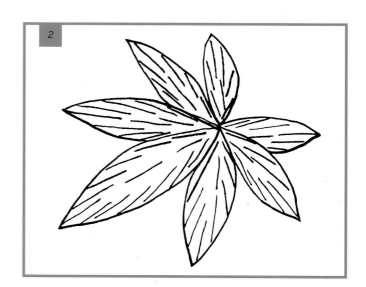

3. ACORN NUTS

Stem stitch the stalks in copper heavy metal no. 12. Split stitch around acorn nuts using one strand of 822, then infill the areas with long-and-short stitch tapestry shading using single strands of 822, 613, 612, 611 and 610. The cups will be completed later.

4. ROWAN BERRIES

Stem stitch the stalks in copper heavy metal no. 12. Split stitch around each berry with one strand of 321. Work a satin stitch layer of padding in each berry using two strands of 321, horizontal to the berry and just inside the split stitch outline. Now satin stitch each berry with vertical stitches using two strands of 321, going over the split stitch outline. Add two tiny chips of old gold rough purl at the top of each berry, stitched with invisible thread.

5. LAUREL LEAF

Work the tapered stalk in rows of stem stitch packed closely together in copper heavy metal no. 12. Complete the leaf in stacked fly stitch using a single strand of 470 and one thread of copper heavy metal no. 30 in the needle at the same time.

6. CATKIN

Stem stitch the stalk in rows of copper heavy metal no. 12. Embroider the catkin with long irregular straight stitches radiating out from the stalk using champagne, sunrise and lime green 371 threads.

7. MAPLE LEAF

Stem stitch the stalk and veins of the leaf in copper heavy metal no. 12. Couch the outline of the leaf in dark brown 3-ply twist stitched down with invisible thread. Complete the leaf with shaded chips of dark brown rough purl no. 8 in the centre, followed by dark copper rough purl no. 8; finish with light copper on the edge of the leaf.

8. OAK LEAF

Leaving 2.5cm (1in) tails at the start and finish, couch the outline of the leaf with dark brown 3-ply twist stitched down with invisible thread. Embroider the inside of the leaf in continuous couching using nut crunch 371 thread stitched down with invisible thread (see **8a** in the diagram below left). Make sure there are no gaps between the rows for a natural finish. Couch dark brown 3-ply twist to form the veins over the top of the 371 thread (see **8b** in diagram below right). Be very careful when plunging not to split the 371 thread.

3. ACORN CUPS

Complete the acorns by outlining the cups in dark brown passing couched down with invisible thread. Fill the cups with long chips of brown wire check purl.

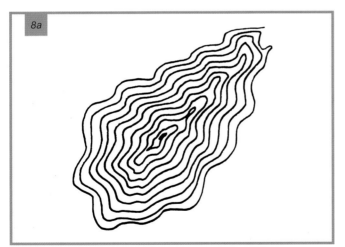

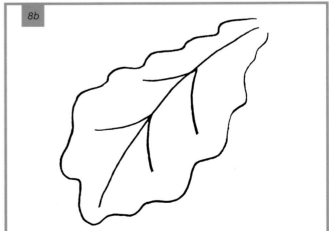

Robin

Hazel hadn't started a design for winter and just had a couple of suggestions as to what to do, so I felt compelled to embroider a robin. This was for two reasons: first, they are synonymous with winter; second, many people believe that robins embody the spirits of people we have lost, so it feels appropriate to finish the book with this in mind.

FABRIC

- Ice blue silk dupion: 20 x 30cm (8 x 12in)
- Calico: 20 x 30cm (8 x 12in)
- Felt: 5 x 5cm (2 x 2in)

THREADS

Robin:
- DMC stranded cotton: 919, 310, 920, 927, Blanc, 921, 3865, 922, 612, 3024, 938, 647, 746, 610, 422, 611, 646

Branch, snow and leaves:
- Brown 3-ply twist: 1m (39in)
- Brown passing: 7m (276in)
- Copper heavy metal no. 12
- Silver smooth purl no. 8: 25cm (10in)
- Silver rough purl no. 8: 25cm (10in)
- DMC stranded cotton: 3012
- Copper heavy metal no. 30
- Invisible thread

TECHNIQUES

- Split stitch (see page 60)
- Long-and-short stitch natural shading (see page 64)
- Bullion knots (see page 76)
- Straight stitch (see page 75)
- Satin stitch (see page 75)
- Stacked fly stitch (see page 75)
- Couched threads (see pages 36–38)
- Fuzzy effect (see page 32)
- Felt padding (see page 20)

TEMPLATE

See page 191

ORDER OF WORK

1 Transfer the design onto the fabric using your desired method and frame up with the calico backing.

ROBIN'S BODY

2 Start with the robin, as she is going to be worked in long-and-short stitch natural shading. Begin with area no. 1 (see diagram **2a** below left). Outline the front and bottom part of the cream belly area in split stitch using one strand of Blanc. Working from the bottom up so the stitches look like feathers and lie naturally, fill in this section with long-and-short stitch using single strands of Blanc, 3865 and 3024, shading where appropriate. For the first row, take the stitches over the split stitch outline and finish with an uneven line to enhance the look of feathers. Complete the area, working towards the red breast. Using the red breast line as just a guide, take some stitches up to, over and under the line to form an irregular, natural-looking line. (Refer to diagram **2b** for the stitch direction.)

3 Now move onto area no. 2. Split stitch the bottom edge with one strand of 647. Then, working sideways and upwards towards the red breast area, work the upper grey/cream area, adding 647 to the mix. Complete this section in the same way as area no. 1, taking some stitches up into the red breast area; this makes sure there is no obvious line between the two sections.

4 Split stitch along the bottom of area no. 3 with one strand of 746, then fill using 422 and 746, again overlapping area no. 2 so there is no hard line. Work upwards towards the red breast.

5 Embroider the red breast (area no. 4): split stitch the outer bottom edge using one strand of 920 then fill the area with long-and-short stitch using single strands of 927, 921 and 920, shading where appropriate. Make sure you take the stitches well into the long-and-short stitches in area nos. 1, 2 and 3 to give a very uneven line.

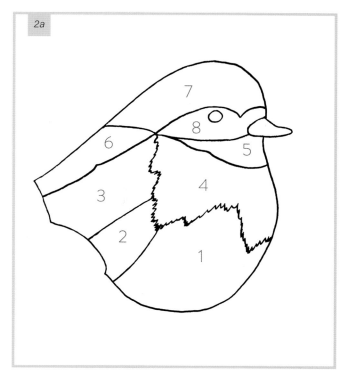

6 Embroider the chin area (area no. 5) using single strands of 919, 920, 921 and 927. Split stitch the bottom edge first, starting with the darkest red then moving up to the beak. Again, make sure your stitches go well into those in area no. 4 so there is no hard line.

7 For area no. 6, split stitch around the two sides of the wing in 611. Then long-and-short stitch the area using 610, 611, 612, 647 and 646, starting from the bottom edge; work towards the head and, when you reach the line for area no. 7, leave all threads here to continue later. Add a few stitches over the top of the join between area nos. 6 and 3 in the colours used in area no. 3. This will help the wing look more natural and the join less harsh.

8 Split stitch around the top of the head towards the beak (area no. 7) with 611. Long-and-short stitch using the threads left from area no. 6 (use 610, 611, 612, 647 and 646). Be very careful with the direction of your stitches in this area.

9 Finish the face with the reds: 919, 920, 921 and 922. Leave a hole for the eye. Make sure you take the stitches well into the other areas to make sure there are no hard lines and so that the sections all join together naturally.

10 Split stitch around the eye in Black and then satin stitch horizontally across it. Add a tiny stitch in 3024 for a highlight.

11 Split stitch around the beak in Black. Use long-and-short stitch to complete the beak – use Black plus 647 for highlights.

LEAVES

12 Add one layer of felt padding to all leaves numbered 2 in the design (see the diagrams below). Add two layers of felt padding to all layers numbered 3. Embroider each leaf in stacked fly stitch using copper heavy metal no. 30 and one strand of 3012 in the needle at the same time. Work all the no. 1 leaves first, then no. 2, and finally no. 3.

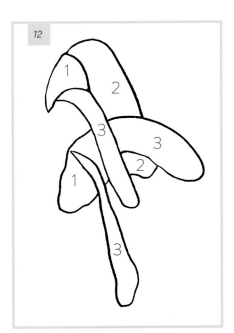

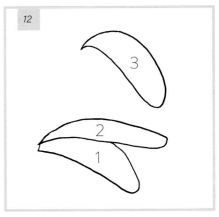

THE BRANCH

13 Embroider the branch in rows of couched brown 3-ply twist, brown passing and copper heavy metal no. 12 to add texture. Stitch down all the threads with invisible thread. Remember to leave tails at the start and end of each thread to plunge and stitch back behind the embroidery when you have finished. Couch one row of brown 3-ply twist along all the outside edges, then, working from the top down, couch two rows of brown passing, one row of brown 3-ply twist, two rows of brown passing, one row of copper heavy metal, four rows of brown passing and one row of copper heavy metal. Fill in any spaces left with brown passing.

THE SNOW

14 Using silver smooth and rough purl no. 8 stitched down with invisible thread, cover the top of the branch and the leaves in fuzzy effect. This can be as thick or light as you like; I have kept mine very light as I didn't want it to detract from the branch and leaves.

ROBIN'S FEET

15 Use two strands of 938 throughout. Embroider the feet by sewing three bullion knots for each foot (see diagram, below). Add a vertical straight stitch at the bottom of each bullion knot to form the claws. For the front foot only, add two small horizontal bullion knots above the three to form the joint, and then three straight stitches under the body for the leg.

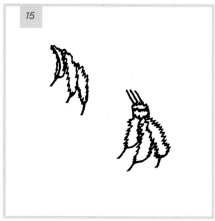

15

Templates

GOLDWORK VIOLET
SEE PAGES 52–53

**GOLDWORK
WILD ROSE**
SEE PAGES 50–51

**SILK SHADED
WILD ROSE**
SEE PAGES 66–67

SILK SHADED VIOLET
SEE PAGES 68–69

LEAVES AND TWO 2D PETALS

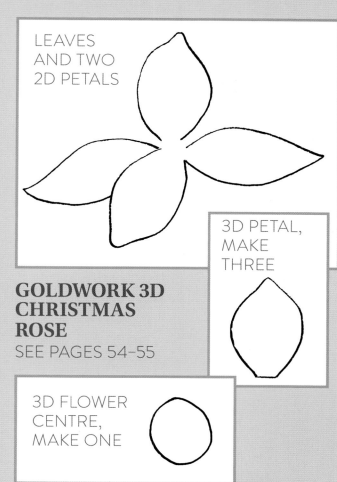

GOLDWORK 3D CHRISTMAS ROSE

SEE PAGES 54–55

3D PETAL, MAKE THREE

3D FLOWER CENTRE, MAKE ONE

SILK SHADED 3D CHRISTMAS ROSE

SEE PAGES 70–71

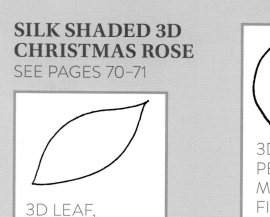

3D LEAF, MAKE TWO

3D PETAL, MAKE FIVE

3D FLOWER CENTRE, MAKE ONE

COMBINED VIOLET

SEE PAGES 80–81

3D PETAL, MAKE FIVE

COMBINED 3D CHRISTMAS ROSE

SEE PAGES 82–83

CENTRE AND TWO LEAVES

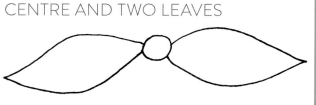

FLOWERS SAMPLER
SEE PAGES 84–93

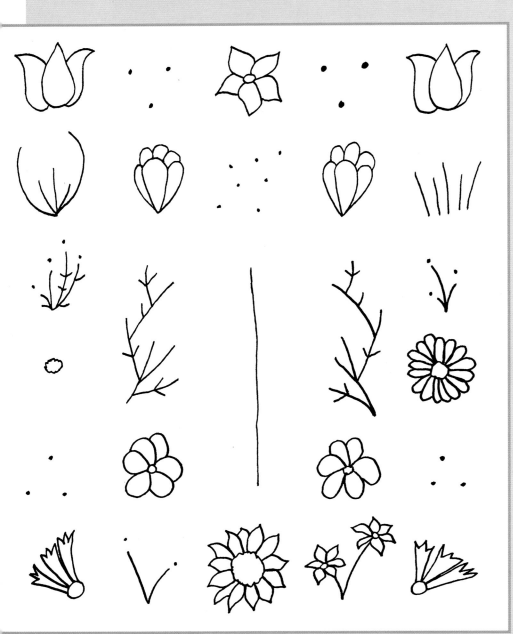

COMBINED WILD ROSE
SEE PAGES 78–79

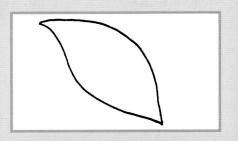

EXPLORING A SIMPLE FLOWER
SEE PAGES 94–95

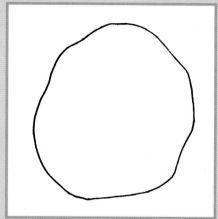

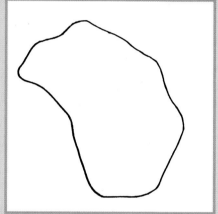

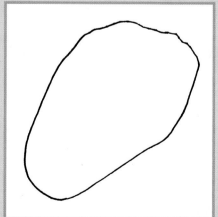

GOLD AND SILKWORK IRIS
3D PETAL TEMPLATES
SEE PAGES 96–98

TREES SAMPLER
SEE PAGES 100–103

177

BONSAI TREE
SEE PAGES 106–107

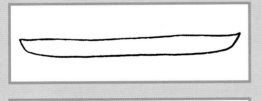

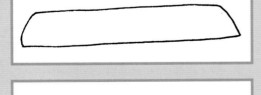

BONSAI TREE
3D ELEMENTS
TEMPLATES
SEE PAGES
106–107

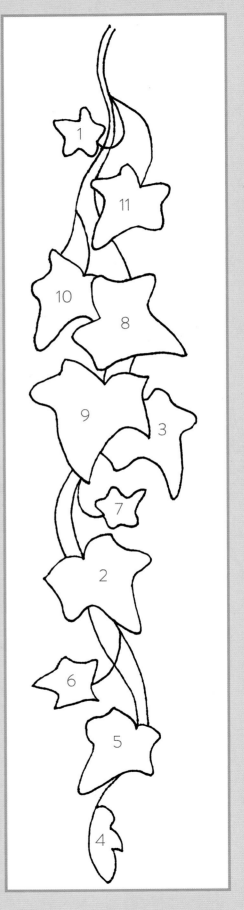

ONE LEAF, MANY WAYS
SEE PAGES 114–115

BERRIES AND SEEDS SAMPLER
SEE PAGES 116–123

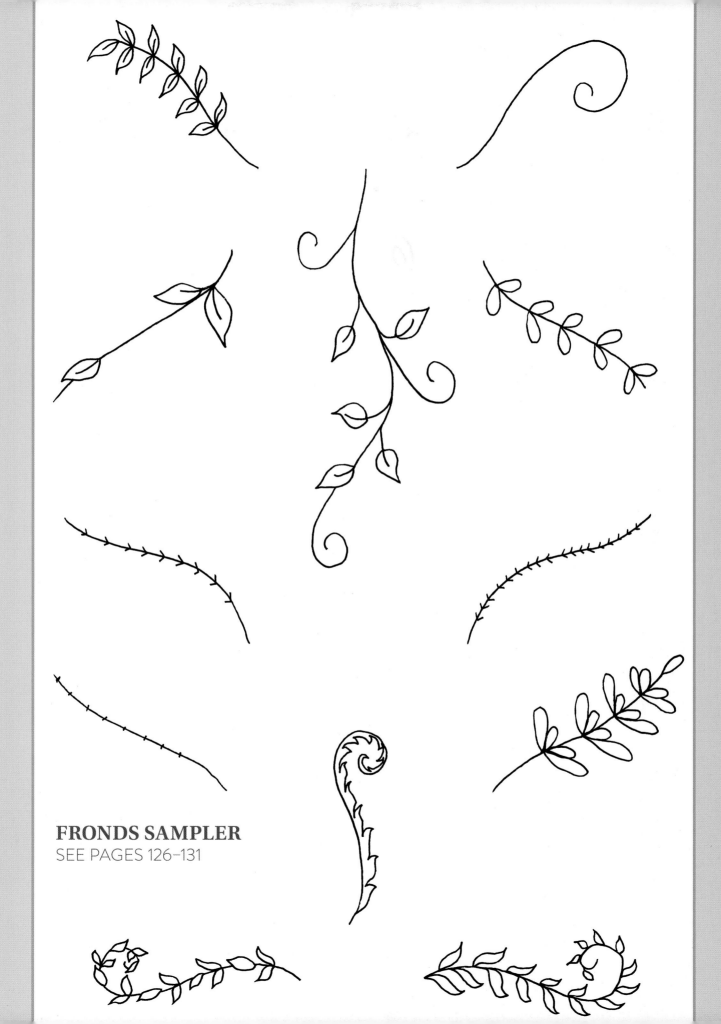

FRONDS SAMPLER
SEE PAGES 126–131

FUNGI SAMPLER
3D SILK TEMPLATE (LEFT);
3D FELT TEMPLATE (RIGHT)
SEE PAGES 132–137

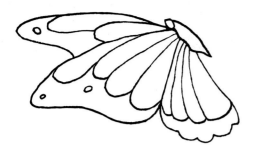

THREE BUTTERFLIES

3D BODY FELT
TEMPLATES
SEE PAGES 138–141

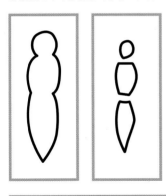

THREE BUTTERFLIES

3D WING TEMPLATES
SEE PAGES 138–141

THREE BATS
SEE PAGES 144–145

ACORNS
SEE PAGES 124–125

BAT
SEE PAGES 146–147

3D GOLD AND SILKWORK
BUTTERFLY
SEE PAGES 142–143

BATS
SEE PAGES 148–149

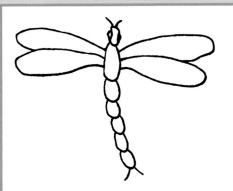

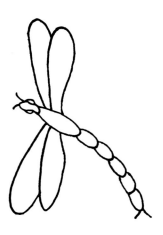

SILKWORK DRAGONFLY

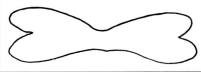

GOLDWORK DRAGONFLY

COMBINED DRAGONFLY

THREE DRAGONFLIES
3D WING TEMPLATES
SEE PAGES 150–153

186

LARGE DRAGONFLY
SEE PAGES 154–155

LARGE DRAGONFLY
3D WING TEMPLATE
SEE PAGES 154–155

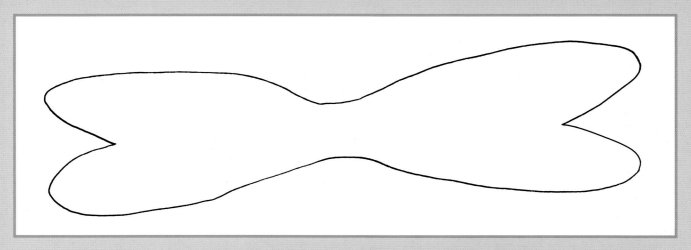

AUTUMN
SEE PAGES 164–167

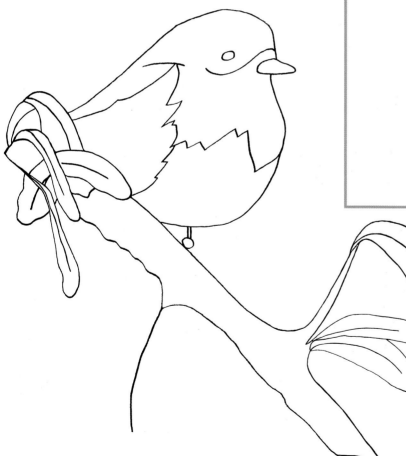

ROBIN
SEE PAGES 168–171

Glossary

Beading needle: an extremely long, fine needle.

Beeswax: used to smooth out and strengthen the working thread.

Bracing needle: a large needle with a spear-shaped, curved point.

Bright check purl: a shiny, multi-faceted edged, hollow thread that is threaded through like a bead.

Broad plate: a strip of flattened metal.

Bump: a soft, loosely twisted thick thread that is used for padding (similar to soft cotton thread).

Carpet felt: a form of padding.

Check thread: a thread with a close zigzag appearance.

Chenille needle: a sturdy needle with a sharp point, good for taking ends through.

Cord winder: a tool that resembles a hand drill with a hook attachment, used for making cords.

Crewel needle: a slender needle with a long eye and sharp point.

Crimped plate: a flat, metal ribbon that has been passed through a crimper/ribbler, creating a corrugated effect.

Curved needle: a semi-circular needle useful for working on rigid surfaces.

Cutwork: the technique of cutting lengths of hollow purl and attaching them like satin stitch to cover an area.

Elizabethan twist: a very fine 2-ply twist.

Embroidery needle: another name for a crewel needle.

Emery cushion: a small cushion containing abrasive powder used to clean needles.

Flatworm: a couching thread with a flattened appearance.

Grecian twist: a manufactured twist made by alternating shiny and matt threads.

Heavy metal thread: a very fine metallic sewing thread.

Imitation Japanese thread (T numbers): flexible, muted-coloured couching thread.

Japanese thread (Japs): a brightly coloured couching thread that is less flexible than imitation Japanese thread.

Kid: a soft leather.

Lizardine/lizerene: a metal thread consisting of a continuous spiral with a straight, shiny appearance, similar to pearl purl.

Mellore/mellor: a specialist tool for goldwork with a pointed end and a flat paddle.

Milliary: a delicate-looking thread with a filigree appearance.

Milliner: another name for a straw needle.

Ophir thread: a 3-ply metallic sewing thread.

Or Nué: a style of design on a background of metal threads worked methodically in one direction.

Passing: a very flexible metal-wrapped thread that can be couched or stitched in the needle.

Pearl purl (PP): a firm spiral thread that has the appearance of a tiny row of beads.

Plate: a smooth, flat metal ribbon.

Plunging: taking the thread through to the wrong side of the fabric.

Pounce: powdered chalk or charcoal used to transfer a design.

Pouncing pad: a roll of felt used to rub pounce through a pricking.

Pricker: a tool to make holes through tracing paper, used in the prick and pounce method of transferring a design.

Pricking: the design punched out with a series of tiny holes, used in the prick and pounce method of transferring a design.

Pricking mat: a spongy foam mat used for pricking.

Rococco: a textured couching thread with an undulating appearance.

Rough purl: a straight matt thread that is hollow and can be threaded through like a bead.

Sharps needle: a slender needle with a small round eye and sharp point.

Smooth purl: a shiny hollow thread that is threaded through like a bead.

Stiletto: a pointed tool, like a miniature poker, for making holes.

Straw needle: a long, slender needle with a round eye and sharp point.

Tail: the raw end of a thread that needs to be left overhanging the design line for plunging later.

Tapestry needle: a sturdy needle with blunt ends.

Ultrasuede: a fabric that does not fray and is ideal for three-dimensional work. Usually used in teddy bear making.

Velvet board: a board covered with velvet, used to cut purls on.

Whipped plate: a strip of flattened metal that has been bound with a fine metal wire.

Wire check purl: a matt, hollow metal with a faceted, textured appearance.